HELLO, MY NAME IS PABST

BABY NAMES
FOR NONCONFORMIST,
INDIE, GEEKY,
DIY, HIPSTER, AND
ALTERNA-PARENTS
OF EVERY KIND

HELLO, MY NAME IS PABST

MIEK BRUNO & KERRY SPARKS

THREE RIVERS PRESS
NEW YORK

Published in the United States by Three Rivers Press, an imprint of the
Crown Publishing Group, a division of Random House, Inc., New York.
www.threeriverspress.com
www.crownpublishing.com

Three Rivers Press and the Tugboat design are registered trademarks of
Random House, Inc.

Library of Congress Cataloging-in-Publication Data

Bruno, Miek.
Hello, my name is Pabst / Miek Bruno and Kerry Sparks
p. cm.
1. Names, Personal.   I. Sparks, Kerry.   II. Title.
CS2377.B76 2012
929.4—dc23   2012012859

ISBN 978-0-7704-3593-6
eISBN 978-0-7704-3594-3

Printed in the United States of America

BOOK DESIGN BY ELINA D. NUDELMAN
COVER DESIGN BY JESSIE BRIGHT

10 9 8 7 6 5 4 3 2 1

First Edition

TO MOM, DAD, AND RICK, FOR GIVING ME MY NAME

—Kerry

TO MOM AND DAD—EVEN THOUGH I CHANGED THE NAME
YOU GAVE ME—FOR GIVING ME SO MANY OTHER THINGS

—Miek

contents

CONTENTS

CONTENTS

CONTENTS

INTRODUCTION

It's just a perfect day: You're sitting in the park, sipping a Stumptown soy latte and reading the latest issue of *Utne Reader* as your little one bounces around on the jungle gym. The sun is shining, there's not a cloud in the sky, and a busker is playing Lou Reed tunes on a saw in the background—but far enough away to enjoy without being annoyed. Eventually it's time for your child's weekly knitting class, so you put your magazine away into your Rough Trade tote bag and wait for the busker to finish his song so you can holler to your child and make all the other parents jealous of what an awesome name you picked out.

But then the record scratches, the busker hits the wrong high note, and another father hollers to his child instead, "Gravel, time for your artisanal-baking playdate with Petunia and Zazzle!" *Gravel? Artisanal baking??* Damn, that's cool. How could this happen? How could someone else be a cooler parent than *you*? You dejectedly mutter your kid's name and usher him off the playground.

Sound familiar? Yeah, we had that nightmare, too, and we want to help. So . . .

Hello, welcome to our book. If you are looking for the perfect funky name for your little tyke, are looking to add pizazz to your own name, or just love to read name books,

Hello, My Name Is Pabst has something for all you indie, geeky, DIY, hipster nonconformists out there. Want your baby's name to be the envy of flannel-wearing, cheap beer–drinking, leg-warmer-clad, ping-pong-playing zombies everywhere? Read on.

FIRST THINGS FIRST

First, choosing a name for your kid sucks. How do you pick just one? How do you name someone you've never met? What if he has an outie belly button? Your kid is going to have to live with that name for the rest of his life, hear or say it a dozen times or more per day, write it down in e-mails, read it in e-mails, maybe even have it plastered on the side of his own food truck one day. And then when he dies it'll be carved into some granite gravestone for centuries to come, where all of his fans will make pilgrimages and leave lipstick kisses and bottles of whiskey, because even though you didn't succeed at becoming a rock god, classic author, and/or the next Warhol, your kid will, you're sure of it.

On top of that, people are coming up with the most awesome friggin' names these days. It seems every month we get an announcement with news that another friend has just one-upped the last with an even cooler name: Haze, Indiana, Tree, Gant, Minnow. . . . It kinda makes you want to just drop being indie altogether, move back to the suburbs, and name your kid Jacob or Emma like everyone else out there. But you're too poor to keep up with the suburbs, and you look awful in khaki anyway, so you really don't have a choice.

We're here to save you. We see this book as the remedy to the "damn, I wish I'd thought of that" pang you get every time one of your friends, Facebook friends, or second circle news feed Facebook friends scores an awesome, heretofore-unheard-of name. Obviously, all the cool kids are having fun with baby names, so c'mon, just try it.

Picking the right unconventional name, whether you're looking for something strong (Hercules, Jett, Hammer), unique (Jazz, Tink, Biv), or happy-go-lucky (Lindy, Felix, Percy), can be quite enjoyable. The more you play with different options and start looking in familiar places for unfamiliar names, the more likely you are to find a fit that is just right for your new addition. This is something you get to do only a few times in life, if that, so have some fun, get creative, and, whatever you do, don't tell your parents what you've chosen until the baby is born, the birth certificate is filed, and the baby is actually in the same room so you can tell them to stop screaming at you—they're disturbing *the baby*.

The goal of this book is not to just give numerous name examples, with alphabetized and gendered list after exhaustive list of names to choose from. We've looked at those books, and we know that you're in such a numb trance by the time you get to the letter *B* that you'll name your kid anything just to get it over with. (TRUE FACT: This is why there are so many Brians and Brianas in the world.)*
While we have a bunch of lists in this book, and it would be awesome if you used a name from one, we also know

---

* Not actually true.

that there's no better mold-breaking name than one from your own imagination. So in each category we'll suggest enough names in the spirit of that category to get your brain working and hope that it will inspire you to find the right one for yourself. The direct connection won't always be immediately obvious (of course surely *you* will always get it), but it is often simply evocative of that category. Sometimes we split each category into different groupings, ranging from more classic ones that we think are still cool to more outrageous ones that take a bit of bravery to go along with. Other times we split them up according to different subcategories within the category, and other times we don't separate them at all, or just pull out the more outrageous ones at the end. C'mon, it wouldn't be a nonconformist baby name book if we actually stuck to one structure, would it? Whatever your passion is, we're certain there's a great name to be found in it that will hold a special meaning for you and doesn't just slip into the blur of all the other kids in the class.

TIPSTER: Hey look at me, I'm a tipster. I'm like a tip, but for hipsters. Get it? I'll occasionally pop up throughout to offer strategies to use and places to search for snazzy names. And sometimes I'll just point out an alternative to a particular category or point you in the right direction. Okay, bye for now.

SECOND THINGS SECOND

You are clearly a unique soul, so of course your offspring will be, as well. If you picked up this book, we're assuming you've already decided to choose a name that is a bit reflective of this, and you're totally not interested in naming your child Tom or Stephen or Mary or Jennifer. Okay, so maybe your annoying childless friend gave it to you as a gag gift at your baby shower, and you've already decided on Audrey or Maxwell for your little precious. Why are you even reading this then? Secretly itching for something a bit wackier?

Before you come up with a good name, you have to let go of the notion that it *must* be a name you've already seen before. The name doesn't have to come from the Bible (though it can—there are plenty of cool names in there) or from your favorite literary work (though, again, lots of choices). And remember that before anyone ever named their kid Violet or Lily, they were just boring flowers, so feel free to jump on Peony, Dandelion, or Rhododendron. While you may not want to go all out and name your kid something like Balcony, just because you've always dreamed of being able to have one, it's perfectly fine to do so, and that's similar to how other names probably came to be, as well. Sky, Paris, Heaven—these were all someone else's dreams, too. And Balcony is actually kind of a cool name. Balcony Jones—say it out loud a few times, look at how cool it looks. You can call him Balcon or Balc or Cony for short . . . it could work. Because inevitably, whatever name you end up choosing for your kid, it will eventually and almost magically fit him to the point where you can't imagine him being named anything other than Laser or Malm.

Still a bit afraid of the deep end? Because of globalization and the overall use of the Internet, where some people go by screen names more often than their own, it is not as risky as it once was to choose a name that is obscure, invented, or even spelled differently. Gone are the days when your child will be beaten up for being named Wilbur or never invited to prom because you named her Priscilla. Kids have found much more meaningless reasons to bully these days, and if anything, a cool or unusual pet name (think Fox, Bean, Tig) will give your kid more street cred if he is the only person in school with it. And if he does get bullied for the name you choose? Well, heck, you were probably bullied, too, but it only made you stronger, didn't it? It's not as if you really want your kid growing up to be prom queen or quarterback anyway, so feel free to inject some fun, creativity, imagination, and good old-fashioned elbow grease into the process.

But still, in choosing a unique name, there's a difference between a name like Apollo, which is uncommon but certainly accepted, and Vandal, which is just plain awesome but could potentially give your grandmother a stroke. You should decide beforehand just how far to go and consider what the implications could be. There are plenty of normal names that are still strong, unique, and likable—such as Oskar, Rue, Maeve, and Benji. Or perhaps you're being pressured to name the child after a family member but want to get a little crazy. We've got tips for that, too.

That said, in many of the chapters in this book we won't just give awesome over-the-top name examples, but we'll also share some classic and contemporary choices that stand a better chance of getting approval from Grandma.

THURD THINGS THIRD

While we really hope that you are able to name your child something totally unique that you absolutely love, like Beaker, Loos, or Kix, we understand that it could be tough to convince others of your choice. Maybe your partner, parents, or friends are dead set against you giving your kid an original name, because they *just don't get it*. Or maybe you really want to, but you're still afraid to make the leap and take the blame every time another parent asks you to say your son's or daughter's name again because she hoped she heard you wrong. We have a few solutions to this dilemma. You can pick a poseur name instead—a normal-sounding name that disguises an awesome nickname. Sneaky sneak! Or you take a plain name and jumble, add, or subtract letters to create a hybrid of normal and crazy. Check it out.

POSEURS

Two literary examples in this category that we love are Toph from Chris*toph*er in Dave Eggers's long-titled memoir, and Nny from the *Johnny the Homicidal Maniac* comic book. (Too obscure a reference for you? Yeah, duh, that's the point). You can slide the cool nickname in after birth, fight for it to stick, and still have the more common name for the kid to fall back on when he needs to find a job.

The main formula for a poseur name is to pick a multisyllable name and simply pull out one or two syllables that sound or look neat by themselves. A few other examples:

Alexander can be Alex or Xander, but you could try Lexan instead. Allison naturally turns into Allie, but why not Lison? Richard often goes to Dick or Rick, but we like Chard—this one will get you some vegan cred, as well.

THE SWAP/SWITCHEROO

Sometimes the key to coming up with a cool name is to simply switch around a few letters, or swap one out for something else. Our author Miek was born in a family where the other men are named Raphael, Agostino, and Dante, so he always hated Michael and Mike. There were six Mikes in his kindergarten class (seriously . . . out of twelve boys). For most of his life people referred to him as "Mike B," which he also hated, while his brothers got cool nicknames like Rafe and Augie. Jealous much? After misspelling it at the end of e-mails so often, he finally decided he liked it more, and voilà, fifteen years later he still goes by Miek (now more often pronounced like *meek*). Most of the time, people online think he's a girl (like the Danish name Mieke), but he doesn't really mind.

If you find yourself falling in love with a great name but feel it's too common, there are several ways to make it your own and still keep the sound and essence of the name. You can add or subtract letters to find the perfect combination. We suggest adding an *s* at the end, because that will often give you the always cool *zee* sound, and making it plural gives the impression that your kid owns everything! Or if there is already an *s* somewhere in the name, you can replace it with a *z* (Jazper, Maizie), or just slide one in next to the *s* for a bonus effect (Szandy, Nikolasz).

Or try swapping out the first letter for another so that instead of the common Liv or Viv, do Miv or Tiv. A few more examples:

SWITCH EXAMPLES: Jaek, Klely, Jaemson, Kaet, Aurlen

SWAP EXAMPLES: Fara, Melilah, Tesmond, Raya, Sleven, Pamona

ADDING AN S: Coles, Jons, Jills, Drakes, Danes, Sams, Crees

SUBTRACTING A LETTER: Oshua, Marle, Vivia, Patick

In addition, these tips above work in the opposite direction, as well. Maybe you're disgusted by the idea of naming your kid something like Taco, but there's no denying that, aside from the greasy connotation, it sounds pretty darn cool. You can drain out this grease, though, by switching the spelling to Tocko, and can fall back on nicknames like Tock and Ocko.

Point: So while some of the names in this book may seem a bit outlandish, with the right mindset and simple creativity they can work very well.

TIPSTER: CrAZy szPelLinG NMs: pUT CaPS iN wElrd pLAceS, AdDh a fiEW SiiLEnt LEtTerSZ, R jst rmv ll th vwls, nd nm yr bby Ptrck, Jnnfr r Mrg. WoWIE-ZowiE!

FOURTH THINGS ONES AND ZEROES

We know you really want to just dive into the name examples right away, but before you get to those (okay, okay, fine, here are a few to keep you going: Grem, Purdey, Key, Argo, Waverly), there's just one more thing: Please, oh please, consider the interwebs while choosing a name. At some point in your child's life, he will get a Tumblr account and an e-mail address, have to create numerous user names and passwords, and be included on lists and in Google results and whatever other things the www will morph into ten or fifteen years from now—face-recognition goggles that "out" people on the street who don't recycle, personalized storefronts that sell Etsy goods via Internet Object Transporters, whatever the hell Apple comes up with next. By looking back at how the Internet has affected our own generation we can start to see why the name you choose now can have numerous implications further down the Internet superhighway. If you name your child John Smith, for example, he'll never get his own "JohnSmith" user name when signing up for anything. He'll be lost in Google search results among a thousand others with the same name, and his friends will have a hard time finding him online. On the other hand, this can work to his advantage if he does something wrong or embarrassing at some point—much of his life will be archived online, from his second-place finish in the town Easter egg hunt at age three to the tagged photos of him smoking a bowl with his friends in the woods at age fourteen.

TIPSTER: While choosing a name that stands out will make your child easier to find online, if in some way he tarnishes this name with an Internet scandal, it will be difficult for him to leave it behind. A sort of "insurance" against this is to use the name you choose for your child as a middle name instead of the first. You can raise him by calling him by this name, but then he has the option to use the first name as his professional name to keep his personal life more hidden and have it to fall back on if something bad happens at some point and he wants to leave it behind.

LAST THINGS LAST

Okay, we're almost ready to get rolling. Just a quick reminder here to stick around for the epilogue after you've gone through the chapters and selected a few names. We'll share plenty of tips there so you can make sure the name you chose is as unique as you thought it was, and also offer help with last names, renaming yourself, naming your pets, and maybe one more hidden bonus track. So here we go!

NAMES THAT FIT INTO SKINNY JEANS

It's likely that your baby will own several pairs of skinny jeans in her early years. You dream of the day you can give her lessons on how to peel them on and off in less than ten minutes—bonding time! However, not every kid's name can pull off acid-wash, slim-fit denim paired with a worn-in band T-shirt. No matter how styles shift over the years, a name that can pull off skinny pants (and, as many will attest, these are not just for über-skinny people, either!) will always be in vogue.

FOR ALL MANKIND:

Willa, VIV, *IONE*, AMALIE, ***GUY***, Pippi, GENE, ***Kate***, CALLIOPE, Brooke, JACQUELINE, *Elle*

Names That Fit into Skinny Jeans

SKINNY, HIGH-WAISTED, NEON:

Dar, **Jo**, NEV, *Gulliver*, Tess, *SHAY*, **Demi**, **TAMAR**,
RIVER, *Greenly*, **CY**, *KAI*, **SLOANE**, Dev, *RAE*, Lil,
Prim, **BAZ**, Jaks, SLIM, **Pru**

JEGGINGS:

Vette, ZELL, Twy, **MALTE**, Pimm, *SKINNY*, **ICI**,
Cinder, ISLE, Nylon, *DEW*, Penn, IVO, Wither,
PLANK, Nix, **Tinsy**, Legs, *Slender*, **Meh**, *VERTICAL*,
Rip Torn

NAMES FOR YOUR ANIMAL COLLECTIVE

If you love eating meat, are an animal lover in the having-pets way, or simply love to dress up like animals in the company of other like-minded adults, it can be really neat to name your kid after one. Furry names like Bear, Deer, and Wolf are hot right now in the indie-rock world, but there are plenty of other greats who haven't yet hit the charts . . . and don't discount the reptile family just because they are cold and unfeeling. Naming your kid after a warm- or cold-blooded creature makes Halloween a cinch, too.

PETA-APPROVED:

> *BUNNY*, ***BEE***, ***Robin***, **WOLF**, **CAT**, BADGER, **Kitty**, **LARK**, Bear, *NEWT*, ***Fox***, Fawn, EAGLE

Names for Your Animal Collective

OUT OF THE CAGE:

FALLOW, YAK, Caribou, *SQUIRREL*, BISON, *EEL*, **Minnow**, TARSIER, *GATOR*, Bass, *BOA*, Bull, ELK, *ROE*, Alpaca, *Tapir*, BARRACUDA, *IBEX*, *Tamarin*, Lynx, **Dingo**, LLAMA, Lemur

WILD RUMPUS:

SLOTH, Grasshopper, ARMADILLO, Clam, *Gnat*, *JAGUAR*, WOMBAT, Yeti, *MOLE*, **AXOLOTL**, Panther, *Octopus*, Python, *SALAMANDER*, **Mule**, *FROG*, Mongoose, Marmoset, *Antelope*, BUFFALO, *Shark*, DRAGON, Chick, *ROOSTER*, Turtle, *WASP*, MEERCAT, Chupacabra

💡*TIPSTER:* If you want to name your kid after a fish but you don't think she could carry off Salmon or Tuna (that's even a bit much for our tastes), a quick Google search for rare types of fish will give you tons of choices that the average city-dwelling indie parent will not be familiar with. Amago, Elver, Buri, Gunnel, Opah, and Loach are great options for your little guppy.

BURLY-WOODSMAN BABY NAMES

You quickly got sick of plucking your eyebrows, going to the hairdresser once a month to frost your tips, and—gasp—*ironing*; being a metrosexual obviously just wasn't for you. So instead you went the route of an urban woodsman—flannel shirts, Wrangler jeans, a six-month beard, and then a subtle edge like a scarf or some nerdy glasses, just so your boss didn't start to worry you were going hick. Whether your child is a boy or a girl, you can give him or her a hearty edge with a name like one of these.

FIVE O'CLOCK SHADOW:

Skeet, Sparrow, **BUNYAN**, *SUNNY*, EMERSON, BRYSON, Hunter, *COLE*, **Thoreau**, Walden, **ASH**, Caleb, WALDO

Burly-Woodsman Baby Names

THREE-MONTH SCRUFF:

> ARCHER, **PERCH**, Trout, **Angus**, *BANDIT*,
> Colt, BANJO, Django, Cain, Moss, *SCOUT*,
> Antler, TRIM, *HOYT*, **AVERY**, BUTCHER,
> **BENELLI**, PLAID, Sport, *GRITS*, **ARROW**,
> AXE, **Drift**, Oxbow, *ANDE*

YOU DON'T EVEN OWN CLIPPERS:

> DECOY, Scope, **LOOMIS**, *KNOT*, **Mister Twister**,
> *LUMBER*, **BOWIE**, Rapala, YODEL, Stren, **Jager**,
> Shad, **Tackle**, *THIMBA*, Grif, *Lure*, **Ammo**,
> Hound, **Shimano**, WRANGLE, *SWAIN*, Zada,
> **Burdock**, *TRACKER*, ACE, **Mist**, Camo, Sturge,
> CARHARTT

💡**TIPSTER:** For maximum irony, pick a name from the Palin family: Track, Willow, Trig, Bristol, Piper, Paxson, Tripp, Mitchell, Britta, Easton, Van, Chuck, Heath, Indy, Sheeran, Bianca, Faye, or Levi.

NAMES THAT LOOK GOOD PAINTED ON A FOOD TRUCK

There are a few things more important in life than giving your kid a cool name, and two of those things are the appreciation of the value of money and the knowledge to run a successful business. Both of these can be combined by simply choosing a name that will look eye-catching when painted on the side of a food truck. Whether your child grows up to sell tacos, whoopie pies, coffee, or some sort of tasteless deep-fried vegan meat substitute, give her a name that will stand out from all the other food trucks. Or maybe your child will fall in love with an entrepreneur who names his food truck after her (like the modern-day sailboat). Either way, it's good press for your little one.

LONG LINE FOR ARTISANAL ICE CREAM:

> HAZEL, **CLEMENTINE**, Grey, *AXEL*, RAMONA, **Matilda**, Juliette, **Felix**, GINGER, *POLLY*, Gwendolyn, *ADELAIDE*, **Ricardo**, Chip, **Currant**, Alfred, **BERTIE**, Herb, ARTIE, *JOSEPHINE*

Names That Look Good Painted on a Food Truck

VENDY AWARD FINALISTS:

Beezie, **GIACOMO**, SOLBER, **WOOLY**,
Bessie, **Sans**, ALDI, *AGGIE*, Van, *DRASBY*,
SANCHEZ, Castor, **TACO**, *FLORA*, **Baja**,
VENDY, ZEKE, *Judge*, Flannery,
PARC, Britzel, *PHINIZY*

DRUNKEN THREE A.M. KEBAB:

Eurotart, **FIESTA**, Hungry, **Pyro**, *SCHNITZEL*,
FALAFEL, Citation, *WAGON*, **Kebab**, GYRO,
Greasily, Mobile, WHIFFIE, Sloppy, **SKILLET**,
KORILLA, NomNom, **YUMMER**, BarbieQ,
CarnitasSupreme

TIPSTER: Don't want your kid to grow up and run a food truck? Shame on you! But not to worry, there's a world of other professions out there that still call for a cool hand-painted sign or decorative font in the banner. Or you could always go for opposite of what you want and name him Cop or The Man. A few to try: Fisher, Boss, Checker, Potter, Drummer, Tanner, Furrier, Weaver, Mason, Hatter, Goldsmith, Dyer, Tailor, Doc, Jockey, Miner, Roadie, Trucker, Cobbler.

NAMES THAT WILL GROW INTO A MUSTACHE

If you have a mustache, you'll probably want to pass that on to your son one day . . . because it's ironic, you know? Plus, with your hairy genes and a little discipline, he could one day enter the World Beard and Mustache Championships and really make you proud! Get him groomed now with names that a mustache will look awesome on.

HANDLEBAR WORTHY:

Earl, **Odin**, Smith, *GOVERNOR*,
Duke, *Homer*, BRETT, *Arlo*, OTTO,
BUCK, *CLARENCE*, Groucho, *Herbert*,
GEORGE, **Asher**, Dax, *ATHEL*, **SINCLAIR**,
Chaz, ANSEL

MUTTON CHOPS:

> *Pez*, Zippo, **MAGNUM**, *VERDI*, MUZ, Manchu, GOATEE, Walrus, *CUB*, **GUMMO**, Cave, *Mars*, *THURM*, RAM, ***ROLLIE BLAR***

GALS WHO'LL GROW INTO MUSTACHES:

> ***HORTENSE***, Bertha, *LORRAINE*, Dixie, ***Butch***, JD, **ANGIE**, Kath, MARGE, Wilma, PORGY, Fay

TIPSTER: To find more mustache-friendly names, just Netflix all your favorite TV shows from the eighties. Maybe you'll rediscover the next hot fashion accessory while you're at it!

NAMES FOR YOUR FUTURE FIXIE OWNER

Hybrid car? *Please*. Hybrid bicycle? Yes, please! You long ago ditched your department-store piece of crap for a fixed-gear bike with neon rims and have never looked back. Just watching your niece in the suburbs unwrap a Huffy on her last birthday was enough to bring you to tears—how dare they give her a Huffy?! So instead you've decided to give your baby a name that will keep her carbon footprint down and get her up on two wheels before she turns three.

RIDING TO WORK:

TREK, Raleigh, *Marin*, KONA, JAMIS, *EASTON*, Tig, Linus, Soma, *Coast*, A. HOMER HILSEN, FIXIE

Name for Your Future Fixie Owner

RIDING TO THE BAR:

SURLY, Mavic, PRIX, *PEDAL*, **NITTO**, Velo, **Cyclo**, *RIVENDELL*, Schwinn, BIANCHI, Stem, **Cog**, Sugino, **SPROCKET**, Velocity, ORTLIEB, Swobo, **Narifuri**, PAKE, Cinelli, *HOZAN*, **Vittoria**

CYCLO-CROSS CHAMP:

HUFFY, **Dyno**, WHEELS, Gear, **HANDLEBAR**, SPOKE, **SADDLE**, *LOCK*, Helmet, TUBULAR, Endo, DISC, **Chrome**, BRAKES, Steel, Lugs, BULLMOOSE, **Fuji**, Hybrid, **TANDEM**, Polo, SEWUP

NAMES FOR YOUR LITTLE BIRDIE

Face it, there is no more appropriate hipster emblem than the bird. You laughed for hours after watching *Portlandia's* "Put a Bird on It" sketch—those friggin' hipsters!—but take a quick look around your apartment. See all those cute silhouetted sparrows adorning your kitchenware, tote bags, mobiles, and other accessories? And then there's the little swallow in your retro Sailor Jerry tattoo . . . and we won't even mention all those tweets you send throughout the day. Shoot! You are *one of them*. So you might as well just give your baby a bird name, too. Not to worry, there are plenty of bird names that only serious birders would recognize as part of the winged family. Fly away with one of these.

V FORMATION:

Raven, **FINCH**, *SPARROW*, Wren, **GULL**, Oriole, **Heron**, CRANE, Osprey, *HAWK*, EAGLE, Thrush, **MALLARD**, *Bird*

Names for Your Little Birdie

BIRDSONG:

> Adelie, LUZON, Carrion, **Vireo**, *LEWIN*,
> *Triller*, PIPIT, Jacobin, *Sedge*, *IZU*, Sibia,
> MYNA, *DUNLIN*, *SOK*, Tui, BESRA, Aves

MISSING A WING:

> *Sooty*, *RUFF*, **PEACOCK**, MUNIA, Gosling,
> RUDDY, **Toco**, GILA, *Whimbrel*, *SLATY*,
> *GUIRA*, *SITTELLA*, Jabiru, *SCOTER*, **Minivet**,
> HOOPOE, Mulga, *SMEW*

TIPSTER: Don't want a name that can take to the skies, out of fear it might leave you one day? Then pick a name from the streets to keep it grounded and less likely to fly too far from the nest: Gravel, Mud, Twig, Turf, Concrete, Dusty, Rock, Brick, Tread, Puddle, Alley, Stoop, Soot, Shade.

NAMES FOR FREAKS AND GEEKS

Dork has been the new cool for years. Ever since Rivers Cuomo made us swoon by looking just like Buddy Holly and allowing us to unravel his sweater as he walked away, the chunky glasses and sweater vests started flying off the discount racks again, and voilà, dweeb cool was here to stay. Wilbur and Hubert, who used to get swirlies every day, and Myrtle and Elsie, who had their lunch money stolen, are now the smart, sensitive yearbook editors and kids in a band, bound for future moderate success in fashion, theater, music, or the liberal arts. Look no further than to the nerds of our generation and generations past to find the perfect name for your cardigan-, glasses-, tweed jacket–wearing, indie world–dominating kid.

HALL MONITORS:

WENDEL, *CLARENCE*, *BERT*, Wilbur, *SHELBY*, Calvin, Walter, FERGUSON, Gertrude, *Hubert*, *NEVILLE*, Eugenia, *HOGARTH*, Bernice, *EUGENE*, PRISCILLA, *BERYL*, *Reginald*, Erma, GLADYS, Earl, *ESTHER*, Eunice, *SHELDON*, *EDNA*, Melvin

Names for Freaks and Geeks

QUIRKY NEW DREAMGIRL/BOY:

> BUDDY HOLLY, **Prunella**, WALDO, Oscar, RUFUS,
> **Agnes**, ALDOUS, Prescott, PERCY, Sylvester,
> MILLICENT, **Webster**, Barney, **Poindexter**,
> NAPOLEON, Mort, **Petunia**, DARIA, **GORDY**,
> **ENID**, Marcel, **CLIVE**, Jarvis, LINUS, Dirk

POCKET PROTECTORS:

> Geezer, **V-neck**, **Urkel**, McFLY, **WILLOGHBY**,
> EGGBERT, Weez, SWIRLIE, Hall Monitor,
> MILHOUSE, Ebenezer, **Dweeb**, SWEATERVEST,
> **MORK**, NORM

NAMES YOU CAN TAKE FOR A HIKE

You equally love rock climbing, snowshoeing, Burning Man, and the Phoenix family, but you certainly don't identify with the long-haired, stoner, hippie types. Just because you were born for adventure in the outdoors and your child was likely conceived in some tent at a music festival does not mean you are one of *those* hippies. How ironic will it be for your pierced, platinum blond, all-black-wearing kid to be named Sunshine? For the perfect nature-punk name, try one of the following.

DAY HIKE:

Meadow, *WILLOW*, ***Autumn***, River, **Lake**, *Forrest*, Sky, *BLOSSOM*, ***OLEANDER***, LINDEN, Alder, **Grove**, CEDAR, ***Snow***, WINTER, Sunrise

Names You Can Take for a Hike

BLAZING A TRAIL:

MOSS, Boreal, *DEW*, ***PRAIRIE***, Balsam, ***TWIG***, Elk, THISTLE, ***Clover***, Petal, CREEK, Maple, *BIRCH*, ***FIR***, Gulley, **Estuary**, Fallow, WAVE, Hummock, ***GLACIER***, Fen, ***Storm***, Tilia

GO JUMP IN A LAKE:

TREE, Stix, ***Air***, *SPACE*, ***GRASS***, Bog, ***MONSOON***, *STUMP*, TRAIL, ***MUD***, *VALLEY*, Peak, CREST, ***DESERT***, MoleHill, *BRANCH*, Bark, ***Vapor***, ***CYCLONE***, *FUNGI*, Yurt

TIPSTER: Flowers make great namesakes for your little one and can evoke both beauty and quirkiness. To take it further than the usual suspects like Lily, Violet, Dahlia, or Petunia, visit a botanical garden with a notepad in hand. Crocus, Hyacinth, Edelweiss, Azalea, Bluebell, Daffodil, Geranium, Teasel, or one of many others might bloom into the perfect name for your naturally birthed tyke.

NAMES TO RESURRECT WITH YOUR STEAMPUNK TIME MACHINE

You spent months building a steampunk breast pump device and decorating your new babe's room with mobiles made from your great-grandfather's pocket watch and keys from an ancient typewriter, then hopelessly baby-proofed everything in your apartment—are all those gears secured tightly? Any loose straps still hanging around? Now it's time to get out the time machine and bring back the perfect Victorian name for your baby. Aviator goggles on!

PHILOMENA, VERNE, Minnick, Cornelius, JULES, H.G., VOLTAIRE, MERVYN, ADA, Merlin, ANUBIS, GILLIAM, Abney, Vernian, CATHERYNNE, Ekaterina, Sepia, Veronique, NEMO, Bertram, ALETHEA, ARAMINTA, CLEORA, DERYN, Gwendolyn, JESSAMINE, MINERVA, OCTAVIA, Eola, Gideon, TWYGG, ATTWELL, PIERS, PILBEAM, HUGO, Mabel, Lottie, RAULYN, Thomasina, AILEEN, Mollow, BICKERSTETH, CORMORANT, Poly, Verlyn, Piper, Clem, Higgs, CYRIL, Drugo, ADAIN, ZEKE, BRISCOE

TWENTY THOUSAND LEAGUES UNDER THE SEA:

Pneumaticcus, Flux, OBSCURA, VITRINA, GEAR, APOTHEKA, Cephalo, KRAKEN, Klock, Whittle, TELECTRO, CYLINDRA, Zeppelin, Alchemia, Luminiferous

NAMES YOU CAN DRINK AT THE BAR

This section is for those who can't remember much about the night this little adventure started. It probably kicked off with some cans of PBR, and you remember someone ordering a round of Jameson, but then it gets a bit fuzzy, though you swear there was a condom present, at least at some point. Even if the whole thing was a lot less skeazy than that and your pregnancy was planned, you probably fell in love with your partner over a nice cocktail in some after-hours speakeasy where they make their own bitters and the bartender brings out the aroma of the garnish by first setting it aflame. So in either case, alcohol was at the root of how this baby came to be, and so something alcoholic it shall be named after.

FEELING A BUZZ:

COLT, *JACK DANIEL*, Remy, Miller, *Jameson*, Bailey, **BUD**, **STELLA**, Olive, **Cherry**

SLURRING WORDS:

PABST, Hennessey, **BOOTH**, Amstel, BEAMER, Stout, ABSYNTHE, *Cognac*, **JUKE**, JIG, Malbec, STOLI, SOCO, *Seagram*, **Ketel**, GOOSE, **DIM**, Cutty, Sloe, **Oban**, Bass, **EQUIS**, PIMM, Fizz, STAG, **SAUNTER**, PICKLE, Tanq, GREYHOUND, Gimlet, Talisker, **ROCKS**, VESPER

SHITFACED:

DIVE, **TUMBLER**, *Angostura*, Curaçao, *Goldschlager*, JÄGER, Dingy, **Caipi**, **Grauburgunder**, SKEVE, Buzz, LAPHROAIG, GROG, Smash, TAXI, *Pisco*, Bloody Mary, **4LOCO**, Buttery Nipple, Redheaded Slut, **SHITFACE**

💡**TIPSTER:** Headed to Alcoholics Anonymous as soon as you found out you were having a baby, and just too afraid you'll fall off the wagon if you think of alcohol every time you say your baby's name? There are plenty of cool nonalcoholic drink names—take a chug of Squirt, Pibb, Boylan, or Sunny D and see how it goes down . . .

BREW-YOUR-OWN-CRAFT-BEER NAMES

You brew your own beer in your garage and have been doing so since way before it was actually cool. You had your best friend design the labels, and then your other best friend letterpressed them on a special paper handmade from locally recycled materials. After a little bit of forcing on friends and family, your brew is now the talk of the neighborhood—you're even turning down orders these days. So if you don't want to name your kid Pabst or Bud because you would *never* be caught drinking that piss, and you want to give her a name that is more like 8% ABV, look specifically at craft beer for ideas. Bonus: This will mean you have to drink each of the names you are trying in order to make sure the beer is strong, smooth, and stands the test of time.

BRONCK, *STONE*, **HOPS**, Ithaca, *Allagash*, Founders, SCHMATZ, **Amber**, Lager, *Lagunitas*, **HARPOON**, IPA, *OSKAR*, **Cider**, Perle, **DONNY**, *BOCK*, Wagner, **DUNKEL**, BARLEY, Troeg, **Jerky**, *ROGUE*, *Spoetzel*, Bell, **KONA**, *ABITA*, Biersch, **ODELL**, Pokal, *Micro*, **PALE**, Boont, *THUMPER*, **Bomb**, Crispin, FARNUM, *OTTER*, BluePoint, *RedRock*, *SCHLAFLY*, Breaker, **SURLY**, ALE, *BREWERS*

A FEW TOO MANY ALREADY? TRY:

MAGIC HAT, *DOGFISH*, JOLLY PUMPKIN, Smuttynose, **Flying Dog**, Hooker, *DIRTYBASTARD*, *ORIGINAL SIN*, **Kegerator,** Ommegang

NAMES (NOT) COMING TO A THEATER NEAR YOU

You have spent so many hours in dark, crusty art-house theaters that you are secretly thrilled with the new trend of fancy-but-still-indie theater pubs that keep popping up, à la Alamo Drafthouse. You can finally see all the obscure foreign films, newest mumblecore gems, and midnight screenings of *A Clockwork Orange* in a climate-controlled theater that doesn't have that faint smell of barf. Besides, you wouldn't even be having a baby if you and your significant other hadn't sat side by side at the movies a few months ago, watching two slightly better-looking versions of yourself fall in love, then out of love, and then sorta back in love again (but not in a clichéd way, of course). Find a future Independent Spirit Award winner with one of these names.

Names (Not) Coming to a Theater Near You

OLD SCHOOL:

Elia, *BETTE*, **Montgomery**, MAUDE, **Audrey**, Greta, HAROLD, *Citizen*, Otto, **Vivien**, BLANCHE, *ORSON*, Gish, MAYER, *SELZNICK*, *BUSBY*, Stella, **RENOIR**, Fritz, MONTY, *Truffaut*, Kane, **BESSON**, Clarice, **BATES**, **Marlon**, Herzog, ROMAN, *GRIFFITH*

NEW SCHOOL:

SPIKE, Harmony, *AURA*, Malick, LARS, *EVELLE*, DEMME, Parker, SOPHIA, Tilda, **ASHBY**, *AMELIE*, **VIGGO**, DUPLASS, **IGBY**, *SEYMOUR*, Hopper, JONZE, *CASPAR*, CRISPIN, **SOLONDZ**, *MEURICE*, **FINK**, JUNO, Barton, **Coen**, *ENID*, **ALABAMA**, Hi

NO SCHOOL:

THE DUDE, Eraserhead, CHAPLIN, *BOOGIE*, Ferris, Strangelove, **Gooney**, Atreyu, *Fargo*, **LYNCH**, *HEDWIG*, DIVINE, *LINKLATER*, BUST-ASS, Requiem, SLOTH, **MR. BLONDE**, Beeswax, **Keyser Söze**, ***Rollergirl***, Grizzly Man

SIGH . . . WES ANDERSON GETS HIS OWN LIST . . .'CUZ HIS
CHARACTERS GOT COOL NAMES:

ETHELINE, Zissou, Rushmore,
FRANCIS, **Dignan**, *UZI*, **Oseary**,
CHAS, **Dusty**, ASH, Raleigh, ***MARGOT***,
Klaus, *Dirk*, **Mr. Fox**, Bishop,
Moonrise, *Walt*, *Scout Master*,
ROOSEVELT, Izod, **Chef**

TIPSTER: To find an untapped reserve of hip names, rent
some foreign films and sit through the closing credits with
your partner. (It might be a good idea to just fast-forward
through the actual movie, though, or each name will probably end up having a connotation of deep misery and/or
subtle pornography attached to it, and that's not really how
you want to think about your kid for the rest of your life.)
You can find cool names like Halldor, Iskra, Penko, Lala,
and Dezso. This works well, too, with most movies (even
big-budget crap), because often it's the editors or grips that
have the best names, so make sure you watch the entire
scroll and keep in mind both first and last names can work
wonderfully.

ON-THE-ROAD-
TRIP NAMES

Living in an urban indie enclave has its benefits—the quirky bars and cafés, cheap international eats, rooftop parties, art galleries, vintage shops, and offbeat jobs that you can brag about. But life never tastes as sweet as when you ditch all those adornments for a few days or weeks, hit the road, and see how beautiful America really is: the wind in your hair; the mountains, valleys, deserts, and coasts; the greasy diners; the gas station nachos; the world's largest puzzle store (think of the kitschy knickknacks you can bring home with you!). Naming your kid after a gas station is an ironic choice for someone who believes so strongly in green energy, but if you plant the travel bug from birth, maybe she'll include you in her family vacations once you hit retirement.

FULL TANK:

ROAM, GETTY, Shell, *Racer*, AKKO, *Cash*, TREK, Esso, SMOKEY, *Cassady*, **ARBY**, *Jethro*, Stone, *Dixie*, Montana, *River*, PILOT, **CODY**, *Sal*, **RUSTY**

HALF TANK:

> *Toll,* **Yield,** Armadillo, **Rascal,**
> EXXON, **NACHO,** Arrow, DRIFTER, **DIESEL,**
> *Cop,* Petrol, **Petty, LEVY,** Euclid,
> VROOM, *Meep*

RUNNING ON EMPTY:

> HOBO, **MEATLOAF,** *Lynyrd,* **LIZARD,** 20Q,
> Bonanza, *66, Xing,* **Journey,** *Arvie (RV),*
> *Effem/Ayem* (FM/AM), U-Turn, **SUNOCO,**
> **Billboard,** *refill,* Empty, *Mosquito,*
> STEPPENWOLF, **Duffel,** Possum, GAS

TIPSTER: You have a sweet little baby now, so why not give her a sugary name using one of your favorite gas station candies? Rolo, Twizzler, Skittle, Twix, SweeTart, Snickers, and Mamba are all cute as a button. But to give it an indie twist, pick a candy that is no longer in circulation (or hard to find in the store, like all those bands you love). Think Charleston and Big Hunk.

MORBID NAMES FOR YOUR LITTLE GOTH PRINCE/SS OF DARKNESS

All that pink and blue in the baby section is driving you absolutely nuts—where are all the studded onesies and steel-toed baby booties? And why didn't anyone tell you they don't exist *before* you decided to get pregnant??? While the first couple of years may be a little tough to swallow, fear not—there's nothing quite as sweet in life as your three-year-old asking to watch *The Nightmare Before Christmas* just *one more time* before nite-nite, watching her dance along to *The Best of Siouxsie and the Banshees* at age four, or helping your five-year-old apply thick dark strokes of eyeliner for the first time . . . awwwwwwww!

DECKED OUT IN BLACK:

> *RAVEN*, **Voltaire**, *VLAD*, ELVIRA, *Hades*, Lestat, NEVE, JUDAS, *SHELLEY*, **TRENT**, *Trinity*, Ichabod, *POE*, Edgar, POPPY, ***DAMIEN***, BRONTË, *GRAY*, DANTE, ***Nell***, LACE

WEARING A TRENCH COAT:

SIOUXSIE, **LAZURUS**, **Boo**, GIGER, **LUCI**,
Caligari, MURNAU, *Adagio*, Demonia, **Omen**,
Harp, BEELZEBUB, *BETELGEUSE*, THIERRY, *DRAC*,
CORALINE, *PRYSM*, GAIMAN, Lacroix, *H.P.*,
Echo, Azrael, **PANDORA**, *ZEPHYR*, *Chalice*,
EBONY, *ZIMA*, TALON

YOU SO MORBID:

OUIJA, GNASH, **GNARL**, SUSPIRIA,
Ripper, *KLEBOLD*, ZOMBIE, **RAZOR**, *WHISPER*,
Dred, **Lucifer**, Fret, *Jinx*, *Necro*,
GRUE, **KILLER**, *BLOODY MARY*

💡*TIPSTER:* Pack a picnic and your favorite book of spells, and then head out to the nearest cemetery to browse names on the headstones. Better yet, bring a Ouija board along and let the spirits name your baby for you.

NAMES THAT CAN ROCK A BONNET

Look in your closet. It's likely there are several peasant blouses, a pair or two of suspenders, long skirts, flannel shirts, and lace-up boots that are more Laura Ingalls than Doc Marten. And if you own a bonnet or a knitted shawl, well, there's no question of your frontier-leaning style. So why not give your baby a name that won't trip over her flowing skirt? Dig out the history books, your old Oregon Trail discs, and VHS copies of *Little House* for some inspired prairie names.

SWEET PRAIRIE:

Della, KETTY, Harriet, *Greer*, *Blanche*, **HESTER**, *TRUDY*, Mimi, Dabbs, *Prairie*, *GOLDIE*, Ginny, *NATS*, **Elmer**, Claxton, *Willa*, **DAKOTA**, NELL, Lucille

NAMES THAT CAN ROCK A BONNET

LOADING UP THE WAGON:

Lolo, Astor, LEM, *DEWEY*, Grassle, *TINKER*, OXEN, Canyon, *BASIN*, Lemhi, GROVE, *CALAMITY*, **LODE**, Sioux, *ORA*

MEASLES, SNAKEBITE, DYSENTERY:

TYPHOID, **Frontier**, *TERRAIN*, **BUFFALO**, Plague, *DOLPH*, BODMER, Dredge, **Pacific**, Rush, MINER, *TRAIL*, *MERIWETHER*, **Teton**, Wagon, *RAIL*, **Plateau**, Fur, **Trapper**, Cholera

ITSY-BITSY NAMES
TUCK IN YOUR TOTE BAG

There is no shortage of tote bags in your closet—the indie bookstore tote, the one with the obscure band patches ironed on, the Andre the Giant one, and of course the tote you got for your twenty-five-dollar donation to NPR—and while your chiropractor has advised against carrying so much weight on one shoulder, you simply can't give them up. What are you supposed to do, wear a backpack everywhere? No, thank you. Pretty soon, you'll be toting around a six- to eleven-pound human anyway, so you need a cute name that's compact enough to fit in a tote.

FOLD 'EM UP, PACK 'EM IN YOUR MODCLOTH TOTE:

ARNO, MIRI, Clem, TUMI, **Logo**, IDA, Hank, Esme, **MAE**, THEO, Isla, SALLY, **Leo**, **Romy**, LUCA, CLIFF, Luna, Polly, **Ned**, Blu, LOIS, WYM, PURDY, Tull, **Devi**, ZOLA, ARGO, Mari, **SAYER**, LISSY, Galo, PEPA, MAVI, DERI, Teo, Odin, **LOMO**, MIDI, **BITSY**, ADA, Buji, Gio, **JEM**, **Jute**

TIME TO BUY A ROLLER BAG:

CANVAS, Fade, *RECYCLE*,
NPR, OOKY, Glove, **Tote**,
KEY, *BOHO*, Cash, Laptop,
Umbrella, Novel, *Calendar*,
Note, *lock*, **WALLET**,
NALGENE, DirtStain

NAMES TO GO WEST, YOUNG ROCKABILLY

So while you've never actually been on a horse, you've been to SXSW and you can rock a pair of cowboy boots and a rattlesnake belt better than most ranchers in Texas. You drink cowboy coffee with whiskey, like to shock your dinner guests with an ironic Frito pie appetizer, collect vintage belt buckles, and host a weekly spaghetti Western movie night. Or maybe you are more rockabilly chic with your punk-rock jean skirt and plaid button-down, square-dance club membership, and love of *Butch Cassidy and the Sundance Kid*. Either way, there are plenty of "out West" names for your little bumpkin.

SATURDAY NIGHT JAMBOREE:

SHANE, *Clyde*, SISSY, Eddy, *Mel*, Doris, **Billie**, VIC, ***ALICE***, Bonnie, Monroe, ***Pearce***, *Delmore*, *Buck*, HANK, *Sonny*, Wanda, *Crawford*, Jacy, *Clint*, Cloris, ***Bud***, ***MERLE***, *Royce*, LYLE, *Roscoe*

COWBOY UP:

> MEADE, Lux, West, MASON, Dixon, Rider, Wyatt, Maddox, RIZZO, Colt, Hud, EVERLY, Lundy, Wilder, BOZ, DAY, NELLIE, Strother, RANCE, BALLOU, NASH, RANGER, Dorsey, Clu, Crosby, LADD, Alis, WALKER, Rebel, Decker, TEX

THE BUCK STOPS HERE:

> Bulge, RAZZ, WADDIE, Slicker, REMUDA, Woolie, Moon, DUST, RODEO, ALAMO, SPUR, Swing, Jamboree, MAUPIN, SADDLE, Jazebell, Travolta, RIFFLE, VELVET, Honky, Cochran, TROTTER, Pony, WOODSY, Equine, BUCKAROO, Cowpie

SECONDHAND BABY NAMES

There are great stories about the deals behind every object in your apartment and every piece of clothing you wear, and your friends are probably a little sick of hearing them. Like a hunter who kills his own meat, you have a special appreciation for everything you own—which flea market/yard sale/thrift store you found it at, who you were with, the rush you got when you first spotted it, and how little (if anything) it cost you. You wouldn't trade in those one-of-a-kind memories for any one-size-fits-all megastore experience, and you want to feel the same about your baby, so try on some of these great name finds.

Dime, **Tag**, Paisley, ***PICKER***, BETA, Canon, PINCHER, *Buckle*, **BEAN**, ZENITH, **Argyle**, Flea, *COPPER*, **Patch**, CASSETTE, Knob, *Levi*, Tool, *MITT*, *Roach*, Lee, LP, Nikon, **BIN**, Zipper, *Magnavox*, **BUGGY**, BROCHE, Tong, *MONOCLE*, Soldier, *Pan*, Crutch, **Clearance**, STARCH, Razor, *KED*, TY, Houndstooth, Pee-Wee, Fringe, PENTAX, Velcro, Patch, **Tiffany**, Stereo

GOT IT FOR A DOLLAR, HONEY-BOO-BOO:

Trashy, *Tchotchke*, Thimble, 8 TRACK, *Super 8*,
Misc, *Tupper*, Zippo, Bazaar, Pleat, **DANK**,
High-Five, Crusty, **Crapola**, Pee-Stained
(THESE LAST THREE WOULD MAKE GREAT TRIPLETS!)

VEGAN AND GLUTEN-FREE NAMES

There are plenty of cool names out there that are all-natural and organic in origin, without the slightest trace of animal or human association. Who wants to give their kid a carnivore name like Todd or Whitney—those are people names, and people are made out of meat. Get your animal-friendly tot ready for a life of clean living with these healthy options (gluten-free names will not be indicated with an *).

SPICES:

BASIL, **THYME**, Sage, CAYENNE, Nutmeg, *Saffron*, *Turmeric*, Cinnamon, CARDAMOM, MINT, Paprika, TARRAGON, **SUMAC**, Parsley, *Betony*, MACE, **DILL**, CLOVE

VEGAN AND GLUTEN-FREE NAMES

GRAINS, SEEDS, AND BEANS:

MAIZE, EMMER, Rye, AMARANTH, DURUM, Semolina, **Quinoa**, KAMUT, **MILLET**, Barley, **Flax**, Adzuki, Fava, LIMA, Spelt, MUNG, Teff, **Caraway**, FARO

FRUITS:

JUJUBE, Tamarind, DRUPE, GUAVA, MULBERRY, **Pear**, Plum, Lychee, Kiwi, Apricot, Acai, **Durian**, Mangosteen, MELON, **Cherimoa**, Sapotes, PERSIMMON, **LEMON**, CITRON, Yuzu, Gooseberry

VEGETABLES:

Sweetpea, OKRA, Chard, KALE, Cardoon, **OLIVE**, SOY, PEPPER, **Miso**, KELP, **Arugula**, COLLARD, RABE, **CHAYOTE**, SAVOY, SORREL, **Radicchio**, Purslane, CRESS, Burdock, TARO, Jicama, CROSNE, Fennel, Cassava, **MOREL**, Brussels, Sprout

FAUX MEAT AND CHEESE SUBSTANCES:

TEESE, **Tofu**, Seitan,
Tempeh, DAIYA, *MORNINGSTAR*,
TOFURKY, Boca, **Tofutti**,
QUORN, Cheezly

VEG CHAMPS:

GANDHI, Fanny, **KEMBLE**, Watson,
Elsie, **Nimmo**, Parsi, *MORAN*, **Peta**,
Silverstone, ORNISH, *EVOLVE*, **Edenic**

TIPSTER: Not sure naming your kid after a food or spice is quite your style? Maybe you aren't a strict enough vegan for this. How about a vitamin or an herb? Browsing the supplement section at your co-op is a great way to find inspiration for names: Maca, Senna, Hyssop, Gotu, Myrrh, Fo-ti, Vitex, Uva, Kudzu, Molasses—or simply Vitamin.

NAMES FIT FOR A SIDESHOW

It happens to all young outcasts—they wake up one day in their middle-class suburban cul-de-sac tract house and realize they just don't belong. They're different. They just don't feel right about the color of their hair, the fact that they weren't born with metal rings through their nipples, that their skin tone is so . . . even. They try to voice this feeling and correct the flaws that nature left them with, but no one truly understands. It's a tale as old as time, and the only real solution, of course, is to run away and join the circus. Whether your little one dreams of becoming a geek, pinhead, or bearded lady, here are some names fit for a sideshow act.

STRANGE BUT TRUE:

PETUNIA, VAUDE, *BEATRIX*, Arturo, *Arty*, Vincenzo, *HERCULES*, **Barker**, *CONEY*, *PUNCH*, Judy, *CHICK*, *THORA*, Tilly, Marietta, *PIP*, *XERXES*, KIT, *PEANUT*

Names Fit for a Sideshow

MARVEL OF MARVELS:

ZOLTAN, Iphy, **Phroso**, ROLLO, *Eck*, OLGA,
Enzo, Apollonia, *Gecko*, Kootch, **ANATO**, *Eltie*,
BLINKY, Hervey, **Wallenda**, Hoppi, ELY, **Thumb**,
Oly, **Hoag**, TOAH, Vivalla, *CLEVE*, BOSCOE,
Zabo, FROZO, **OSCA**, ASRA, Apexia, *Omi*,
Gomper, Kroger, MYRNA, *Rasmus*, Delno,
NATHAL, *Lobsterboy*

YOU WON'T BELIEVE YOUR EYES:

NORVAL, Fredini, ALBINO, Cotton Candy,
Tetrallini, *Lodz*, STUMPY, Lizardio,
ZIGUN, Schlitzie, **Ringmaster**, *Demetrio*,
Banzai, **Wilno**, Pinella, *Barbella*, ALZORIA,
LIPKO, **ZENOBIA**, ZRIBEDA, **CLIQUOT**, Zinida,
Krinko, *Eeka*, Percilla, **Zenora**, *Rocketman*,
Trapezo, **THE GREAT**

THESE ARE THE NAMES IN YOUR HIPSTER NEIGHBORHOOD

Young parents are reinventing the idea of naming children after a generically lovely place, leaving behind played-out names like Savannah and Paris for more in-the-know place names like Portland or Berlin. But the fewer people who live there and the harder it is to find, the better, so be sure to look outside the familiar realm of big cities and countries—there are plenty of street names, bodies of water, establishments, and even general directions that can make for terrific names. To get you started, here are some names inspired by the indie-dreamer enclaves across the U. S. of A.

BROOKLYN:

BQE, Prospect, MARCY, Beastie, *BEDFORD*, MEEKER, *Kellogg*, Elle, DRIGGS, **Wythe**, Stuy, *Armory*, **GREENWOOD**, NAVY, Verrazano, Dumbo

These Are the Names in Your Hipster Neighborhood

PORTLAND:

POWELL, *BURNSIDE*, **Huber**, ROSE, Couch (pronounced Cooch, duh), **Multnomah**, *WILLAMETTE*, *Pearl*, Gus, *BLAZER*, Max, **Stark**, Forrest, **HOOD**, *VOODOO*, PDX, *COIN*

AUSTIN:

BATS, Sixth, BARTON, **TOWNE**, Saxon, *RANSOM*, *HILL*, Travis, **Hays**, Capitol, *LONESTAR*, **VIOLET**, *ALAMO*, SXSW, Balcones, Hyde, **Lamar**

DETROIT:

Pontiac, Cadillac, *8 Mile*, BERRY, *GORDY*, DIA, Von Bondie, **PISTON**, Cass, *WOODWARD*, Hamtramck

MEMPHIS:

Eggleston, **Beale**, Stax, **Sun**, *GRACELAND*, **Shelby**, Wharton, *Cooper-Young*, *Levitt*, Booker, Dixon, *ODESSA*, **PINKNEY**, Rhodes

SILVER LAKE:

Echo, RESERVOIR, Sunset, JUNCTION, Mix, **Hyperion**, Griffith, ***VIRGIL***, *HERMAN*, East, *Neutra*, FELIZ, Gaulke, Glen, ***Socal***

NEW ORLEANS:

NOLA, Levee, ***GRAS***, Quarter, BORGNE, Ward, BAYOU, *DELTA*, Tulane, *JAZZ*, Praline, Tanker, ***Jambalaya***

SANTA FE:

Desert, GEORGIA, *Zelanzy*, Tobey, ***Cactus***, PERCY, *BYNNE*, **Zozobra**, *TAOS*, Caldera, ***Adobe***, Mirage

SEATTLE:

King, *MERCER*, ***ELLIOTT***, Puget, *PIKE*, ***UDUB***, Boeing, *TIMBER*, Cascade, *MADRONA*, *TULLY*, Haller, ***LESCHI***, QUEEN, Ravenna, Renton, *MARINER*, Kent, ***SEWARD***, *EMERALD*

These Are the Names in Your Hipster Neighborhood

SAN FRANCISCO:

Farallon, **HAYWARD**, Irving,
Fillmore, ALCATRAZ, Nob, *Ferry*,
Lombard, **Fog**, *Berkeley*, *Coit*, BAY,
Ashbury, MARIN, **Baker**, QUAKE,
Breaker, GAYE

O CANADA:

TORONTO, Scotia, **Vancouver**, Montreal,
Winnipeg, MANITOBA, Kamloops, *Saskatoon*,
OTTAWA, Timmins, **HALIFAX**

NAMES THAT WORK NO MATTER WHERE YOU LIVE:

DELI, *Street*, **ACRE**, AVENUE,
Crater, **BRIDGE**, *North*, Lake, **Alley**,
LANE, Dogrun, DRIVEWAY,
CarWash, DINER

♀ TIPSTER: Live off the map? To find even more place names, pull your globe out and start spinning. Wherever your finger lands, that's your kid's name. Hudson Bay has a nice ring to it. Or, try dusting off your atlas and start browsing through it for small-town names. Focusing on cities will more likely land your kid with a common name, so check out low-population places, county names, and rivers. The options are almost endless, but here are few gems we love: Penza, Anvers, Muncie, Ukiah, Bossier, Amory, Coulee, Missoula, Moberly, Hoquiam, Abilene, Elyria, Harlan, Borah, Huron, Eucla, Benin, Rainier, Lulea, Cebu, Tuxtla, Guilin, Biscay, and Elbe.

NAMES THAT COULD ROCK A MIRANDA JULY HAIRCUT

Miranda July is a renaissance woman. She makes art, writes books, directs films, pens screenplays, and acts in her own movies. And through it all, she's always sporting the perfect haircut—an effortless looking bob with wispy curls and bangs—and the perfect old-lady fashion . . . we're talking pussy bows, folks! It's every parent's dream for his or her little girl to grow up into such a well-rounded woman, so why not start her off with a name that can really rock a good Miranda July haircut or just evoke awesomeness. It's just one small baby step toward eventual obscure-yet-critically-acclaimed-and-oh-so-arty greatness . . .

ME AND YOU AND EVERYONE WE KNOW:

Florence, **Mabel**, SOPHIE, Delilah, MADGE, Daphne, LUCILLE, **DOTTIE**, Josephine, MAEVE, **ELEANOR**

NAMES THAT COULD ROCK A MIRANDA JULY HAIRCUT

NO ONE BELONGS HERE MORE THAN YOU:

Maisie, SOOLEY, Minnow, **Beck**, *Teala*,
IVY, Cleo, *RAND*, PERCY, *MIM*, ***FINLAY***,
Embry, **JONI**, LINDY, *ROONEY*, Tillie,
ELODIE, Len, *Orly*, JULY

THINGS WE DON'T UNDERSTAND AND ARE DEFINITELY NOT GOING TO TALK ABOUT:

TWIG, ***KIX***, Sailor, FERN, *RUE*, Pluto,
Tootsie, *Petula*, Bumble, *GALO*, **Snow**,
Kleep, *BLOOM*, **Joanie4Jackie**, *Snarla*

SCARY MONSTER (AND SUPERCREEP) NAMES

Names like Chastity, Grace, and Truth make you want to puke hard. You're drawn to the dark side of things, love scary movies, and savor the rare occurrence of watching the good guy lose, but most of all you simply *hate Twilight* for making vampires so damn cheesy . . . I mean c'mon, glittery skin?? No thanks—you'll take watching an original print of *Nosferatu* down at the art-house film series any day. While you don't want your kid to grow up and become a bad guy, you definitely think it'd be cool to name him after one. Here are some cool villain names.

CREEPY AND KOOKY:

Chucky, **Damien**, EBENEZER, *BATES*, HILDA, Igor, VLAD, Addams, *HAL*, Blair, **SWEENEY**, **CARRIE**, SZANDOR, *JACK*

SCARY MONSTER (AND SUPERCREEP) NAMES

MYSTERIOUS AND SPOOKY:

Lestat, *GANON*, Lurch, *BOOGIE*, **JARETH**, STRYKER, *Mystique*, Cruella, **DARTH**, **Desdemona**, *DRACO*, FESTER, **MORTICIA**, *KONG*, **Dusk**, Gage, **HOOK**, Scar, *URSULA*, GRADY, *SAMARA*, Torok, Gein, *KEFKA*, **FINKLE**, *Everglot*, **Hatter**, WESKER, *RIPLEY*, *SAURON*, Bundy, Gremlin, Hyde, *VITO*, **Rodan**, KAEL, **JADIS**

ALTOGETHER OOKY:

HANNIBAL, **SASQUATCH**, **Amity**, It, **FLY**, Leatherface, *Pinhead*, *JIGSAW*, **Sniper**, **OOGIE**, MOTHER BRAIN, Sephiroth, Skek, *GLaDOS*, XAYIDE, **The Nameless One**, **X**, *Godzilla*, *Mothra*, Gmork, **Garthim**, Baumorda, **Adele**

NAMES THAT FLIP YOU THE BIRD, THEN SPIT IN YOUR FACE

Your kid is gonna be so punk rock, and that's a fact. Forget the No More Tears shampoo—you'll be using bleach and green hair dye on your baby's scalp and sending invitations for her first piercing instead of first communion. As far as you're concerned, the answer to "Mommy, can I skip school and stay home to play my drums?" is *"Hell, yeah!!"* Whether you like the old sound or the new sound, you should give her a name that will make the other mommies and daddies cringe.

ONE SNOT ROCKET:

Iggy, DeeDee, **SID**, *NANCY*, JOHNNY, Debbie, Blondie, **Lars**, Vivienne, IVY, *SPIKE*, PATTI

TWO SNOT ROCKETS:

Anti, *SNOT*, RAMONE, **CBGB**, GUTTER, Anarchy, *Pogo*, *RANCID*, *McLaren*, *FILTH*, **LABRET**, Tragus, *SEPTUM*, **Slik**, *DEXY*, **Mosh**, *Slam*, Zine, JELLO, *Proto*, *STUD*, Bromley, *TROUSER*, Taper, **Plaid**, Pin, **Crust**, Bum, **ACID**, Thunder, *VOIDOID*

THREE SNOT ROCKETS:

Doc Marten, *VICIOUS*, Droog, **Prol**, OiOiOi, THE BIRD, *BUZZCOCK*, SKANK, **STRANGLER**, **CHUMBAWAMBA** X-RAY, *BEG BORROW STEAL*, Rotten, *Fury*, Misfit, *SPIT*, LOOGIE, **Snarl**, Little Bugger

NAMES YOU CAN SPELL, PUNCTUATE, AND CALCULATE

Sometimes the best names are hiding in the letters, numbers, and punctuation that we use every day. Saul Hudson completely rocked his new name, Slash, and who can forget funky-fresh Blossom's best friend, Six? Not all numbers and letters will work, so choose carefully: Seven will always be cool, but we're not sure Two will ever really work; names with the letter *z* in them are automatically cooler than those without; and obscure-punctuation-related names work better than Period or Exclamation.

THE LETTER Z:

ZSA ZSA, *PEZ*, Beezus, **ZAX**, *ZORRO*, **Roz**, Zola, Zevon, *PEREZ*, *Zuma*, *LOZAN*, *ZILIA*, BOAZ, **Kazir**, *ZED*, **Zephir**, Enzley, Zuriel, *Bazel*, ZEUS, ***Dweezil***, *Kinzee*, Zerk, **ZINDY**, *SZANDOR*, CAZLEY, ***Paiszley***, Zappo, *Izac*, KEEZER, *Zuza*, Fez

NAMES YOU CAN SPELL, PUNCTUATE, AND CALCULATE

COUNT MY NAME:

> **SIX**, *FIVE*, TRES, ***TWELVE***, Seven, *Century*, **OCTAL**,
> YEARLY, Decimal, Quinary, *BASE*, Prime, Numeral,
> *UNO*, Dos, ***LAKH***, Crore, KANUM, *SKO*, **Api**

PUNCTUATE BABY:

> *TILDE*, **Caret**, *Bullet*,
> Ampersand, ***DASH***, *Comma*,
> **Obelus**, Colon, *Slash*, ***Asterisk***,
> Guillement, GRAMMAR, *PARENTHESIS*,
> Bracket, Dotcom, DECIMAL,
> *Apostrophe*, ***HYPHEN***, ELLIPSIS

💡*TIPSTER:* Instead of naming your child after punctuation, you can also try incorporating some into your kid's name: Ada could become Ada!, :Ada:, or A*da. Or just name the baby after an emoticon ;-P :-X You so cr@zy . . .

NAMES FOR NIHILISTS

Why does a name have to mean something? We're only here a short time, life is meaningless in the grand scheme of the universe, and there's nothing cooler than pretending you just don't care anyway. Rebel against all those straights trying so hard to come up with an original name by naming her after nothing at all. Or just name her Nothing At All. As in, Nothing At All Jones.

ZERO:

Zip, ZERO, *Zilch*, NULL, **NADA**, Void, **Nothing**, *Nix*, NAUGHT, Zot, **Scratch**, Blank

LESS THAN ZERO:

NIHIL, **NIL**, **Nietsche**, **CAMUS**, DEARTH, *REBEL*, *TURGENEV*, Stranger, **Kafka**, *Kierk*, *SISYPHUS*, **Infinity**, *Gregor*, *FYODOR*, Zarathustra

DOWNWARD SPIRAL:

ANONYMOUS, **ANON**, *DURDEN*, Din, *DADA*, **CIPHER**, Moot, *Nebbish*, *UNSPECIFIED*, UNKNOWN, Whatchamacallit

NAMES THAT KICK ASS ON THE ROLLER DERBY TRACK

You found out you are having a girl, and you plan to raise a strong, independent, powerful woman who doesn't take any sh#t! If you throw her in some roller skates and give her a kick-ass name, she'll be drinking hard and getting into fistfights in no time. Okay, well, maybe you'll need to work on that side effect a bit . . . but adopting Roller Derby naming methods can be a great way to find a cool moniker for your strong gal (or guy, to really throw everyone for a loop). Really, why go with Kate when you can go with BackAlley DaBlockerKate? If that's a bit too extreme for you, here are some other inspired names.

UP ON SKATES:

MIDGE, DERBY, ***LaRue***, *DIXIE*, *Betty*, Carolina, *Aurora*, **Marjorie**, **Josephine**, BRYNN, **Darla**, *Bonnie*, Trixie, *Farrah*, Gertie, ***Jackie***, GILDA

Names That Kick Ass on the Roller Derby Track

JAMMERS:

HELLENOR, **SKELLY**, *Kyller*, Gammon, Brasuhn, BOGASH, *SELTZER*, **RUNYON**, Murray, VEGAS, **Diamond**, CALVELLO, Rollz, Crimson, LEXUS, **POP**, *Ozzie*

WHIP-IT:

ELBOW, DIVA, *Renegade*, JAM, *RENO*, Guard, *Block*, **Dame**, DOLLZ, *BRAWL*, ZOOM, *Bruiser*, SAUCY, *SMACK*, Hammer, **ASSIE**, *AlterEgo*, Bombshell *BLOCKER*, SavageGrace, JACKASSJEAN, Badass *(INSERT ANY NAME HERE)*

TIPSTER: Still want something a bit more feminine? Take whatever name you please and just add *-ette* or *-ella* to the end. This works to make a normal name unusual (Rachelette, Lynnella) or the most drab objects into gems (Tarpette, Bulbella).

EASY-TO-ASSEMBLE IKEA NAMES

What better name for your child than the piece of furniture he was conceived on? Don't think of it as cheap, low quality, or disposable, but rather stylish, distinctive, and extremely popular. This is the perfect way to give your little one a unique name with just a whiff of familiarity, so you'll always remember that hot night of conception. And years later, when he moves into his first roach-infested warehouse loft in Detroit, furnishing will be a cinch—heck, maybe this naming style will be the beginning of a new family tradition!

Haven't made the baby yet? Buy whatever name you and your partner like most, get a to-go order of Swedish meatballs to really set the mood, and then head home and start cranking those allen wrenches, baby . . .

MISSIONARY ON A BED OR SOFA:

> *MALM*, **BIRKE**, HOPEN, Oppdal, ODDA, **Mydal**, Tullsta, HUGLO, *LATT*, Hogt, **Hallen**, Sultan, *HOGLA*, **EKTORP**, *Poang*, Hovas, KLOBO, *MUREN*, *PELLO KLIPPAN*, *SATER*, Agen

Easy-to-Assemble Ikea Names

HANKY-PANKY ON THE KITCHEN TABLE, CARPET, OR COFFEE TABLE:

Pragel, *Flytta*, INGO, **Norbo**, **UTBY**,
SALMI, Bjursta, GRANAS, *Lanni*, Melltorp,
Torsby, KAUSTBY, **BERTIL**, Nisse, EGIL, *INGOLF*, SKAR,
DAGNY, BALSER, Balum, Dragor, EGEBY, Gatten,
GASER, **Gislev**, Havbro, **HESSUM**, HULDA, KARBY,
Ludde, KOGE, Morum, Blom, Rens, FILT, **TARNBY**,
Vitten, **VALBY**, **Adum**, BOKSEL, LACK

BENT OVER A BOOKSHELF:

GRONSKA, Svalen, **BILLY**, Benno, VALBO, Laiva,
VALVIK, DIODER, Lagra, **VATE**, Basisk, TORNA,
SODER, **Foto**, MINUT, STRANNE, Alang, Asele,
BOJA, Fado, FILLSTA, **AROD**, Forsa, Grono,
GYLLEN, Lunta, **Skirma**, JANSO, Jonisk, BARBY,
EGBY, KNUBBIG, **Gryby**

NAMES FOR YOUR SO-CALLED LIFE

You likely learned many of your life lessons from eighties and nineties television shows—how to sneak out of your bedroom window, how to shun your beliefs in order to be cool only to learn the *real* you was better all along, and that every house should have a stairway in both the living room and through the kitchen. Plus, who could forget all the canned-laughter catchphrases like "Dunt! How rude! Did I do that?" Shows like *Growing Pains*, *Life Goes On*, *Saved by the Bell*, *Roseanne*, and *My So-Called Life* give you tons of possible names for your baby.

WHERE EVERYBODY KNOWS YOUR NAME:

HARRIETTE, *Kimmy*, Six, HAYDEN, *Peggy*, Murray, *Banks*, **BLOSSOM**, *Clarissa*, Griffin, ***Daria***, LILITH, *Trent*, Baily, *Rayanne*, CARLTON, ***CYBILL***, *Norm*, Fox, Darlene, Estelle, *Vivian*, DYLAN, Mona, *LEON*, Walsh, **Woody**, *Beverly*, *WINNIE*, ***Tanner***, *Bud*, *Murphy*, MIMI

LAUGH TRACK:

Boner, **SCREECH**, Brighton,
NILES, *TOPANGA*, Corky, Slater,
Balki, Winslow, *FRASIER*,
Catalano, MORK, MacGyver,
URKEL, Belding, *KRAKOW*,
Cosby, *Nash*, D'ARCY,
Ferguson, **Seaver**

TIPSTER: Guest stars, secondary characters, and weirdo neighbors tend to have the best names in this genre, so pay special attention to Jackie's long list of boyfriends on *Roseanne* (Booker, Fisher), the recurring characters on *Boy Meets World* (Minkus, Chet), and various coaches on your favorites shows (Paintz, Luther).

NAMES WITH DREADS

Little hippies are so friggin' cute, with their nothing-but-overalls attire, dangly little hair things, and dirty little fingers. They're even cuter when they have those names that come out of nowhere, like Aardvark or Crock-Pot. As the drugs have gotten more potent in the last decades, hippies have become less and less content with Moonbeam, Stardust, and the other go-to names found in nature and have raised the bar on naming their children something completely out of touch with the mainstream. So if you've already shunned consumer culture altogether but somehow just found this book in the middle of a daisy patch, consider some of these neo-hippie names.

CHICKPEA, Tennessee, *Granola*, VOLCANO, **FIG**, *Borealis*, PEGASUS, Patchouli, ***Effigy***, Monday, HUMMUS, *UTAH*, **Firepit**, *VISTA*, Gypsy, *TABOULI*, Neptune, *Bandana*, Vermont, *HITCH*, Compost, BEANBAG, ***Organic***, *SPECK*, Analog, *Volunteer*, CRICKET, **HACKYSACK**, ***ZUZU***, SNICKERS, Flute, ***Pagan***, *QUARRY*

HAVING A BAD TRIP:

Birdmonkey, Tarantula, **Cauliflower**, SATCHELBERRY, **Wormhole**, Couscous, Hawkeye Clampit, THORAX, Serbia

TIPSTER: Don't forget about the middle name(s), too! The key to making a hippie name extraspecial is putting together two or three names that have nothing to do with each other—Gypsy Cricket, Cauliflower Hitch, or Analog Serbia Thorax.

BRAVE NEW BABY NAMES

One of the most popular methods for naming a child has always been the literary reference. Go to a playground in Brooklyn on any given day and you'll feel like you're back in ninth grade again, reading *To Kill a Mockingbird*: "Atticus! Scout! Stop throwing sand at Boo! Dill, please don't chase Harper!" But as popular as this method is, there are still plenty of hidden gems in all your favorite books. Don't feel obligated to choose a noble character—just choose a name that sounds or looks cool. Thumbing through books in search of minor characters is a great way to show off your library again on the subway or in the café. Author names, of course, work well, too, and don't just focus on the popular or classic titles. What better way to show how obscure and wry you are than to name your child Brautigan or Gaddis?

CLASSICS 101:

Sawyer, *Toklas*, **HOLDEN**, *PIP*, Moby, **Auster**, *Oscar*, *Juliet*, **Homer**, *GATSBY*, ***Lysander***, Hunter, *RHETT*, Gertrude, *Percy*, *EYRE*, Wilde, *SILAS*, **BRONTË**, Huck, *Tennessee*, **Djuna**, *MURDOCH*, Magus, Anaïs, Joyce, **Finn**, *ALDOUS*, Heller, *Carson*, **Saul**, Muriel, *Ulysses*, Fury, ***Sherwood***, *TRUMAN*, Toad, **TWAIN**, Nin, *ROTH*, FARBER, *Knopf*, **Godot**

DISCOVERED THROUGH YOUR LOCAL INDIE BOOKSHOP:

KESEY, Carver, GALT, **Roark**,
Zazie, **SUNNY**, Alexie, **FANTE**, *SALTER*,
MUNRO, *EASTON*, Wallace, *Ayn*, YEATS, **Fiver**,
Ripley, *Lorelei*, **GONZO**, *BALLARD*, Chuck,
SALINGER, *EGGERS*, MOODY, McSweeney, *FOER*,
Bukowski, Opus, Bolano, **Didion**, *TOPH*, CHINASKI,
Oskar, **Akashic**, MICHIKO, **ALMA**, Tao, JULY,
DELILLO, Junot, *STEIG*, CORMAC, **SNICKET**,
SALMAN, Hornby, *SALANDER*, Zak, *LYRA*,
Zadie, **DALKEY**, Roddy, *GREIL*

DEVOURED BY BOOKWORMS:

Woolf, **MOBI**, Grendel, KEROUAC, **Eppie**,
SAFRAN, GOGOL, *ArturoBandini*, Zergog,
Kilgore, KINDLE, **ATLAS**, Rabbit, *PORTNOY*,
Wooster, *HEMINGWAY*, EPUB, YabYum,
Vook, EEEE, Humbert Humbert

💡 **TIPSTER:** Reread your favorite childhood books for name inspiration. Characters in children's books tend to be just slightly ahead of the naming curve. Pippi, Lorax, Grimm, or Beezus, anyone?

NAMES FOR YOUR LITTLE ARCHITECT

You say you'll be happy with whatever profession your child chooses when she grows up, but of course you are lying. Secretly you long for her to be an architect—it's that perfect combo of professional but not boring like a lawyer or a doctor, and she might actually be able to pay for your nursing home one day. Plus, she will always look smart and sharp in her architect glasses, all-black attire, and messenger bag. Best of all, your kid will never have to explain what exactly it is that she does to a table full of relatives. (Why can't Aunt Marge comprehend what a production assistant/food truck server/blog curator/performance artist is?) Prep her for a bright future—and a childhood full of elaborately constructed sofa-cushion forts—with a well-designed name.

ASSOCIATE:

MEIER, WREN, **EAMES**, Rosette, GRAVES, **Wright**, *GABLE*, Aldo, *EATON*, **MARCEL**, Sullivan, *ENNIS*

Names for Your Little Architect

PARTNER:

Mies, GEHRY, *Renzo*, **LOOS**, Aalto,
Siza, GAUDÍ, Maki, **Boehm**, Roche, GRUEN,
Barragan, *Botta*, Soleri, **ANDO**, Corbel,
ORIEL, **Lunette**, ARCH, Cornice, *Cella*,
Pratt, RENESE, *Moma*, Kenzo

YOUR OWN FIRM:

Koolhaas, **FLATIRON**, *Angle*, GUGGENHEIM,
Canopy, Eiffel, *Venturi*, *Column*, **Gherkin**,
CALATRAVA, Doric, **Sash**, DIFFA, Dormer,
Buckminster, **Empire**, Sagrada Familia

NAMES FOR YOUR SPIRITUAL BABY

When a friend gave you a gift card to Futures by Marie a few years back as a joke, the psychic told you that you would be a parent in less than five years. You laughed it off at the time, seeing as you didn't even own a couch! She also told you that you would move to a new and wonderful place and realize your full creative potential . . . so one out of three isn't bad. You may not be sold on past lives and all that, but you do get the sense that the universe won't be giving you a regular baby Joe, so find a name that is anything but earthly.

THE STARS ALIGN FOR:

AURA, *Orion*, MOON, *CELESTIAL*, Andromeda, *Lunar*, SUN, *SPIRIT*, WAND, Divinity, *Gem*, OPAL, **ARA**, Crux

Names for Your Spiritual Baby

ZODIAC, MYTH, Tarot, EARTH, **PLUTO**, MARS, Jupiter, *NEPTUNE*, SATURN, Palm, FIRE, Deck, **MEMORY**, Mystic, *Constellation*, Equinox, Solar, *DIPPER*, **Argo**, POLARIS, **Caelum**, Letus, **DRACO**, *Lyra*, **Vela**, Tucana, *VOLANS*, *URSA*

YOUR THIRD EYE IS BULGING:

Chart, **IMUM**, Trionfi, ETYMOLOGY, *HARUT*, **Marut**, Vertigo, **INSPIRE**, *VOODOO*, Past-Life, Path, **Journey**, *NUMEROLOGY*

💡TIPSTER: If you don't want your kid to waste a lot of breath on answering the question "What's your sign?," then just name him after the star sign he was born in. Capricorn, Aquarius, Pisces, Aries, Taurus, Gemini, Cancer, Leo, Virgo, Libra, Scorpio, and Sagittarius all make pretty great names. If your kid is born in early July and you don't think naming him Cancer is very nice, you can always choose a compatible sign like Pisces or Scorpio.

NAMES FOR A MAD SCIENTIST

Okay, there's not much that's cool or indie about science. But you know what *is* cool about science? The names. You probably missed out on these by sleeping through much of your biology, chemistry, and physics classes in high school, or paid attention to them just long enough to fill in a Scantron bubble and then forget them forever. We don't blame you. Take a look at the list below, though, and there's a good chance you'll wish you were naming triplets.

PERIODIC TABLE OF ELEMENTS:

Zinc, COPPER, *MERCURY*, **Tin**, *Tungsten*, **Argon**, Sulfur, *XENON*, Boron, *LITHIUM*, Beryllium, **Cobalt**, Alloy, *MANGANESE*, *Neon*, Krypton

BIOLOGICAL:

HELIX, Amino, AGAR, *Enzyme*, **POLY**, Plasma, **EXO**, ENDO, **DEXTRIN**, Heme, **LIPID**, Tibia

Names for a Mad Scientist

FOUND IN THE LAB:

BEAKER, *BUNSEN*, PETRI,
Checks, PIPETTE, Scope, Micro,
Elixir, Erlenmeyer

QUANTUM MECHANICAL:

TESLA, Boson, **Higgs**, QUARK, Atom, **Ion**,
BOHR, Spec, *FERMION*, Neutron, **Meson**, Proton,
BARYON, *Beta*, **Angstrom**, Gamma, **X-RAY**

WAY IN OUTER SPACE:

ASTRO, *Apollo*,
RADIO, *HUBBLE*, **Vega**, Mars,
SOLAR, DOPPLER, Pulsar, COSMO,
COMET, UFO, Orbit, **Meteor**,
Sonic, *RADIO*, Martian,
ANDROMEDA, *DIPPER*

NAMES FOR A KICKBALL DREAM TEAM

The most ironic thing about your utter dominance of your Saturday kickball league is that you were a complete failure at every other sport your father shoved down your throat as a kid. But now you're *#winning* in your mismatched American Apparel tube socks, vintage Umbros, and fluorescent headband, and have an MVP trophy made of PBR cans to prove it. So give your kid a name that will be throwing fist pumps as soon as he pops out.

HERE'S OUR KICKBALL DREAM TEAM:

Jett, FURST, *Trophy*,
VAN, *Dash*, MOSES, PHOENIX,
WIN, *Champ*, Star, **Kicks**, SPEED,
Paz, **Red**, Base, SLAMMER,
BUNT, Corky, **Torpedo**

Names for a Kickball Dream Team

♀TIPSTER: Don't like to break a sweat but still love a competitive game? Find great names as you kick your friends' asses at Boggle, Scrabble, and Bananagrams over a nice vegan casserole. Not only can you show off your wordsmith skills but you might come across a bunch of name possibilities. Too poor to have real board games? Just make up your own word game by cracking open the dictionary. There are millions of name choices, plus you'll have your definition right at your fingertips. Who needs real sports?

NAMES THAT CAN BE TAGGED ON WALLS AND BATHROOM STALLS

Crayons are meant for walls, not paper. You're such a true artist that you reject the commoditization of art altogether. You believe it should be for the people instead of just the rich and that public space belongs to the public, not the advertisers, even if it's the inside of a dingy bathroom stall. Be sure to exit through the gift shop with these names.

BANKSY, *Blu*, Shepard, *Fairey*, SWOON, Faile, ANDRE, **Blek**, **Undenk**, Inkie, **Krylon**, Kakos, *Overpass*, OS, Avant, BORF, *Scharf*, Celso, Knitta, KAWS, *Spray*, *Krane*, Obey, Samo, METRO, *Meek*, *Phibs*, Vhils, JR, Toof, CYCLOPS, *Bumblebee*, Billboard, *Aryz*, Lemza, STENCIL, *Jaz*, Ludo, **Zilda**, SPECTER, Eine, VANDAL, Ethos, *Hoodie*, *EVOL*, *Sam3*, ZEVS, *Muck*, **NEWFIE**, **Akbar**, Kekko, *Velspar*, **Squid**, Dondi, Daim, *Ces*, Reas, **Espo**, Kilroy, **Belton**, ZEPHYR, *Tats*, ECKO

FREAKY STYLEY:

D*Face, **DLUX**, *Luzinterruptus*, FAUXREEL, *SLINKACHU*, Molotow, ***Stinkfish***, **EARSNOT**, Neckface, PHLEGM, Plunder, REVOK, *SPACE INVADER*, SKEME, Fab Five Freddy

TIPSTER: Opening a box of crayons or heading to the hardware store to get a bunch of paint samples can prove to be a great place to find colorful and obscure names. You can go classic or get wild with it: Mauve, Pink, Lavender, Periwinkle, Azure, Indigo, Coral, Maize, Teal, Cyan, Aureolin, Roy G. Biv . . . just to name a few.

NAMES TO SHOUT OUT AT OPEN-MIKE NIGHT

Your kid will quickly learn that all the liberal arts life is a stage. She begins by reading poetry at an open-mike night in a dingy coffee shop, and then progresses to a one-woman show in a half-empty dive bar, before finally getting her big break after that NEA grant is revoked on account of "indecent content." Despite the seriousness of whatever message your child will ramble on about, you need to give her a name that carries so much oomph that she doesn't even require a last name. Photocopied fliers for a show by Sarah Jackson will just wind up in the gutter, but a name like Xander or Roscoe will easily fill another two or three foldout chairs. When you find a name you like, yell it over and over in front of the mirror like you are introducing your offspring for the first time. Then start rubbing canned yams all over your naked body, just for the fun of it.

WORKING THE CROWD:

FERDINAND, **Gant**, Zane, Malcolm, Joaquin, *BECKETT*, Kingston, ***Andre***, Daschel, Franklin, ***Bruno***, LEOPOLD, *Rocky*, Xander

Names to Shout Out at Open-Mike Night

GOT A GOOD WRITE-UP:

Rinaldi, **DANDY**, Barazz,
Roscoe, Malachai, OLEANDER,
Django, **ZEVON**, CHAZ,
MAGNUS, Candalina, Lakda,
Dizzy, *PHAEDEN*, Thaler

THERE IS NO FOURTH WALL:

ORALLY, VAUDE, *DRIP*,
HONZIK, Myth, **Poet**, Brilliant,
HAZE, *UNDERSTATED*, Vibe, BEAT,
OOPS, Skronk, GLITTER, *HERO*,
Hazard, KUSH, **Soliloquy**,
Shelter, Rambling, *Dumbo*

NAMES FOR A HELLO KITTY LUNCH BOX

When you share your adorable baby name ideas with other people—Moomi, Tiny, Bib—they always use the line "Cute, but you have to try and imagine the kid as an adult, going for a job interview, and going on a matchmaking site. . . ." Blah, blah, blah, blah, blah. Those annoying people are assuming you actually want your baby to turn into an adult! Ick, gross. Want to give her a name that will guarantee she stays cute forever and is still carrying a lunch box and wearing pigtails into her thirties and forties? Try one of these cuties.

HAPPY FUN FRIENDS:

KIKI, *Tiny*, Bunny, Love, Kitty, **Pekkle**, Keroppi, Dottie, *Birdie*, Minna, CHARMMY, Sanrio, **Landry**, Maru

Names for a Hello Kitty Lunch Box

SILLY LOVE FRIENDS:

> Sooley, *BLOOM*, Bipi, **Bop**, *LOMO*, MOOMI, Pochacco, KUROMI, ***CAMOMILLA***, Nao, Mimmy, Yuko, ***POCHI***, BADTZ, Purin, **Kuririn**

KITTY GONE WACKY:

> ***Anime***, Kyd, *BOO*, **Little**, ***BIB***, Deery-Lou, *SUGARBUNNY*, Mimobot, **HAPPY**, Chococat, **Friend**

TIPSTER: Need another super place to look for names? Try doing some Rainbow Brite research! Names like Sorell, Canary, Lala, Murky, Popo, Stormy, Twink, Starlite, Krys, Plock, Orin, Shimmer, On-X, Lurky, Sprite, Zombo, Blogg, and Wajah are colorful gems!

NAMES FOR YOUR FUTURE KICKS ADDICT

The joy of a new pair of shoes is hard to replicate. New-car smell has nothing on that new-shoe smell, and it's unlikely that you'll ever actually own a new car anyway. Though you buy most of your clothes at thrift stores and hole-in-the-wall vintage shops, when it comes to shoes you need a pair that is limited edition, preferably neon, and costs half your paycheck. Show your kid that shoes really can bring together the whole outfit by giving him a cool kicks name like one of these.

SEAVEE, **Toms**, GRENSON, *SEBAGO*, Vaider, **Coogi**, *AXION*, **Ked**, Vulc, *McNairy*, CHUCK TAYLOR, PUMA, *FRYE*, FISK, Converse, One-Star, *Saucony*, OSIRIS, Van, ***ETNIE***, **CLARKS**, Sperry, Burton, *Rogue*, RADII, Mia, *Tretorn*, SUPRA, *Ecko*, RAF, Vox, Duckie, HARDY, Heutchy, **Lugz**, **Emerica**, Globe, *ELEMENT*, *SUPERGA*, Zuriick

THE SHOE FIT . . . SO YOU BOUGHT THREE PAIRS:

SneakySteve, **UGG**, Schmoove, FALLEN, Chukka, *Grenade*, **Gazelle**, Bedstu, *BLUNDSTONE*, ESQUIVEL, **Volcom**, Florsheim, Springcourt, *TIMBERLAND*, Ingelmo, **Generic Surplus**

NAMES TO BE LETTERPRESSED

Even though you own several functioning typewriters, you are still in the habit of sending letters through the mail that you compose on six-dollar handmade cards from a booth at the weekend farmers' market. It's likely that you have even gone so far as to hire a local letterpress artist to make one-of-a-kind birth announcements for your one-of-a-kind baby on the way. If you have the design all set to go but just can't fill in the name, why not look to the history of print for inspiration? There are many cool names that even Johannes Gutenberg would be proud of.

ROLLERS:

Buxley, Mainz, BRASS, *VERSO*, **Platen**, Scroll, *VELLUM*, Tone, Copper, *Ludwig*, ROSIN, Mordant, Hopfer, *PRICE*, Emboss, Engrave, **Chandler**, *Font*, PRESS, *Adana*, Custom, *Anilox*, Glyph, *Ingot*, Graver, *FOUNDRY*, Laser

Names to Be Letterpressed

ALREADY HAVE YOUR OWN KELSEY EXCELSIOR 5×8:

Flong, *Mould*, **ETCH**, Matrix, DUPLICATOR, Mezzotint, **Hectograph**, Rotary, *Vandercook*, Heidelberg, ***CALLIGRAPHY***, INKY, Grayscale

NAMES THAT WILL REACH THE FINAL LEVEL

People put you down for years, making fun of your geeky late-night Quake sessions, your lame arguments over who would win in a fight between Baraka and Kratos (Kratos, duh . . .), and your annoying habit of injecting sound effects into every conversation. It was hard to find and keep a girlfriend for a few years, but you kept playing, and gaming eventually prevailed—you're part of a multibillion-dollar industry now, a sexy mainstream activity, so you won, made it to the next level, conquered the enemy, whatever you want to call it. And so, hell yeah, that fully gives you the right to name your kid Tetris if you want. Break out the Red Bull and celebrate with your joystick into the wee hours—you earned it!

ATARI, ZELDA, Sonic, **Toad**, *RYU*, Scorpion, Kong, Gaiden, Pit, ***TRON***, Raiden, *Pac*, SAMUS, *Metroid*, Bowser, Ganon, Combo, *LINK*, ***KIRBY***, Yoshi, Goku, PONG, *TAILS*, Koopa, *TECMO*, Kitana, SEGA, *Contra*, *Mercy*, MegaMan, Halo, ***Warcraft***, Cloud, PIXEL, Garrett, Arthus, *NUKEM*, Illidan, Kratos, *MINC*, Sephirath, *The Nameless One*, *SHODAN*, Jak, EZIO, ***SPYRO***, Madden, SQUALL, Navi, *Tifa*, **WII**, Moxxi, *WHISPER*, Wesker, ***Cid***, Azel

Names That Will Reach the Final Level

YOUR PRINCESS IS TOTALLY IN ANOTHER CASTLE:

Tetris, **FROGGER**, DIGDUG, Q*Bert,
GALAGA, Centipede, *Fistpump*, ARCADE,
Soda Popinski, **PINBALL**, 1UP, XBOX360,
ALLYOURBASEAREBELONGTOUS, Quarters,
UP-DOWN-UP-DOWN-LEFT-RIGHT-LEFT-RIGHT-A-B-A-B-START,
Oregon Trail

FASHION-VICTIM BABY NAMES

You love your indie culture, we know. But above all the tedious lit, cinema, and music your friends chatter on about, nothing is more meaningful to you than showing off your new outfit or accessory at a well-attended rooftop party, and you wake up at *least* once a month in a cold sweat, having just had that recurring nightmare where you made it to the *Vice* "Don'ts" section—again. Give your kid some style with a name like one of these.

Marc, **SEVIGNY**, Suede, *McQUEEN*, Agnès B, *THIERRY*, Trucker, LODEN DAGER, Commes, Gilt, LABRET, *Rodarte*, Scarf, **WESTWOOD**, *GRANNY*, Headband, Charm, *RU*, Dov, Tavi, **Posen**, MUGLER, Ked, *Leigh*, BARNEY, Gunn, *SUI*, Betsey, *Garçon*, **ROWLEY**, Henrik, *ISSEY*, GALLIANO, **Hedi**, Preen, Charney, *RAF*, Viktor, ROLF, *Mies*, Vera, **ZAC**, Wintour, *FEDORA*, **Vans**, Edie, TOTE

Fashion-Victim Baby Names

PARIS IS BURNING:

Corso Como, SWAG,
Dandy, MULLET, Heatherette,
Acne, *KENNY KENNY,* Jort,
Hush, Shade, SASHAY

NAMES THAT BELONG IN A DIALOGUE BUBBLE

Whether you grew up reading the funny pages and super-hero comic books, longing to one day save the world and get the girl, or you spent that time actually kissing girls and only later on discovered the literary and artistic value of serious graphic novels, you're totally pumped that, with a baby on the way, you'll now have access to a whole new section of the bookstore that's more pictures than words. So give your baby a name that can make you laugh every morning, fight crime, or give an illustrated perspective on the human condition. Be careful, though—these names could end up living in your basement and eating all your cereal well into your retirement years.

FUNNY PAGES:

JUGHEAD, *Schmoo*, ARCHIE, Beetle, *Bluto*, Hobbes, *BLONDIE*, **Dagwood**, Capp, *BLAISE*, Marmaduke, POGO, *Snuffy*, Obelix, Ziggy, *DILBERT*, Doonesbury, Little Orphan Annie

Names That Belong in a Dialogue Bubble

SUPERHEROES:

Captain America, *Tick*, Spawn, MAGNETO, Rogue, *Morpheus*, Mystique, LEX, Xavier, *Dredd*, Y, SWAMP THING, *Hulk*, Pryde, GARRICK, *PEPPER*, **HELLBOY**, Thor, Astro, Mekon, *DR. STRANGE*, Arkham, WOLVERINE, Sabre, *SILK*, **KRYPTONITE**, Kurse, DR. DOOM, *V*, Deena, Mage, *ROBIN*, Halo, **SIF**, Zatanna, **POW**, Bam, Whiz, *KAZAAM*

ART COMIC/GRAPHIC NOVEL:

Derf, DIRGE, **LENORE**, Crumb, Squee, STRUWWELPETER, *Jhonen*, PEKAR, Pilgrim, TANK GIRL, *Clowes*, Gaiman, LEONIDAS, *Dream*, Palomar, **NNY**, Maus, *Spiegel*, *Marjane*, HABIBI, *Grendel*, Noodle, **Thessaly**, VLADEK

NAMES FOR A SATURDAY MORNING

If you have to watch one more episode of *Dora the Explorer* with your niece, you might lose it. All the cartoons these days are so heavy on education, morals, and viewer participation that they seem to miss the whole point of cartoons—all that really matters is a fun-tastic lunch box, a Happy Meal toy, and an iron-on T-shirt. From the *Get Along Gang* to *Thundercats*, and the truly, truly, truly outrageous *Jem*, here are some names from the days when cartoons were a blast and you spent your Saturday mornings glued to the tube instead of nursing a hangover.

QUIMBY, Casper, BRAIN, *Gadget*, Claw, *Marco*, WOOLY, *TAILOR*, **Hefty**, Scrappy, Daphne, **SHAGGY**, Donatello, BEAKLEY, GLADSTONE, *DRAKE*, Beagle, **DEWEY**, *Gyro*, WEBBY, **Merlock**, Gander, *She-Ra*, Josie, PENFOLD, *JEM*, TEELA, *Orko*, Kimber, *JERRICA*, **DINO**, Minx, Gusty, *PACKY*, Snarf, **TYG**, *LIONO*, Jaga, *SLITHE*, PIDGE, ALLURA, *ZANDEE*, Coran, ***BANDOR***, *Gumby*, **Woolma**, Hugsy, SLICK, Flip, *THEKLA*, Kowl, Hordak, Snork, KELP, **Esky**

CONJUNCTION JUNCTION, WHAT'S YOUR FUNCTION?:

VOLTRON, Stimpy,
Sloppy, Shredder, *SPLINTER*,
GoBot, INTERPLANET JANET,
Skeletor, PawPaw, *Slimer*,
PUNKY, *Squakencluck*, Tooter,
Fangboner

NAMES TO CTRL-C AND CTRL-V

You're a serious artist, but you make your money working for the Man as a graphic designer. It's your dream to one day make the transition to the art world, but all your original ideas keep getting shot down because your boss just doesn't want to take the risk/do something different/get it. But whatever—all your art-school friends who refused to compromise are still living in a Bushwick bedbug collective, while you're comfortably paying down a mortgage on a 1,500-square-foot loft in Dumbo, so c'est la vie. . . . Name your kid after your favorite font, program, keystroke, or tool.

CLICK HERE TO DOWNLOAD THE LATEST PLUG-IN:

Typo, GROTESK, **DPI**, PNG, GIF, *JPEG*, Quark, **FAQ**, CLICK, *Double-Click*, Right-Click, CS5, **PINWHEEL**, *Gimp*

Helvetica, *PIXEL*, **COURIER**,
ARIAL, **MAC**, Adobe, Track, *LOFT*,
SHORTCUT, *Serif*, **SANS SERIF**, VERDANA,
GARAMOND, Plantin, DIDOT, Arnhem, *Sylfaen*,
Scribus, COREL, *Perl*, Bevel, *Acrobat*, Arc, FLASH,
CAD, *Logo*, Tonal, RENDER, Linux, *PERL*, *Bitmap*,
Anchor, *SCALE*, Xara, *ETCH*, **DODGE**, Gamut,
Midtone, Zip, ZOOM, Raster, *KERN*, Hue,
VECTOR, **MACINTOSH**

TIPSTER: Ensure that your baby will grow up to love your Apple products as much as you do by inserting an *i* in front of his or her name—iTallulah, iBennett, iMarc, iLila, iCarlo, iEtc . . .

ART STAR BABY NAMES

You've spent so much time guzzling free wine at gallery openings, you probably don't even need this section. It's no secret that artists have always had great unusual names, and some would argue that it's what planted the nonconformist seed in them to begin with. So if your dreams of being the next Warhol have already dried up and you've sold out to the graphic-design world, pick a name that will give your child a better chance at getting a pavilion at the Venice Biennale one day.

GROUP SHOW:

> **Dash**, *TERRENCE*, **CINDY**, NAN, Damien, **ALEC**, Piet, *BARNEY*, Jasper, Cy, *SADIE*, Edgar, *GEORGIA*, JEAN-MICHEL, *Willem*, **Liam**, Eva, *EAMES*, *Agnes*, BORIS, CLAUDE, **VLADIMIR**, STELLA, **Dorothea**

Art Star Baby Names

SOLO EXHIBITION:

> Helmut, **OLAFUR**, **GAVIN**, *Luc*, Walker, **Olaf**, OPIE, *CYRIL*, KLEE, *Marcel*, **Banks**, Collier, GIGER, *Mies*, **LUCIAN**, WASSILY, **Amadeo**, RAPHAEL, *RONI*, **VITO**, **MAURIZIO**, *Rineke*, Anish, *ELLSWORTH*, Sigmar, **PIPER**, Neo, **Kiki**, **LORNA**

CAREER RETROSPECTIVE:

> DARGER, *ANSELM*, Yayoi, SOL, *Shirin*, YOKO, Hopper, **NAM**, On, **Ai**, *WEIWEI*, **Nadar**, **TACITA**, Slava, *Edouard*, Edvard, *DINOS*, RIRKRIT

TIPSTER: Don't forget about art supplies for name inspiration: Gesso, Elmer, Kiln, Matte, Canvas, Easel, Utrecht, Clay, Graphite, Faber, Turpenoid, and Mylar.

NAMES THAT CAN LIVE ON RAMEN NOODLES

Like most slightly directionless, real-world-fearing smarty-pants, you ended up in grad school, a place where you could focus on your specific interests related to environmental legislation, Russian cinema studies, sustainable development, and knitting. You have mapped out the next several years of your life to avoid having to do the unthinkable—get and keep a job. But with a little one on the way and the upcoming expense of cloth diapers and eco-friendly Onesies, you might have to give up the dream, get rid of the futon, and join the ranks of grad-school dropouts. But to keep the memory alive, try one of these.

ZIZEK, DOC, *Ramen*, DERRIDA, **VASSAR**, *OBERLIN*, LOAF, *BADIOU*, Source, *KENYON*, Prescott, **Scholar**, Roland, *THRIFTY*, Argyle, **Zinn**, *WESLEYAN*, WELLESLEY, ***Rushmore***, ***Eugene***, *CHEGG*, Quad, *Essay*, Parson, BRICK, **Journal**, *MARX*, ***Prof***, BUCKNELL, Thesis, MAJOR, Bard, ***Keg***

STUDENT LOANS IN DEFAULT:

Sallie Mae, **ADJUNCT**,
UNI, **Footnote**, *Tenure*,
Swarthmore, *BROKE*, Tweed,
STACKS, HappyHour, **GMAT**, GRE,
Overdraft, SCANTRON

NAMES THAT BANG HEADS AND WORSHIP THE DEVIL

Whether you've moved on from the eighties or are still stuck there, one thing beyond dispute is that Metallica simply *ruuuuuules*. And if it weren't for that damn kid from Seattle with his dreamy blue eyes and candy-ass suicide, we'd probably all still be carving pentagrams into our forearms and biting the heads off bats, and our mullets would be down to our heels by now, if not dragging on the floor behind us. And hell yeah, it'd be so friggin' gnarly (in a good way). Honor the gods and slaves of the underworld with a kick-ass heavy metal name.

Metallica, *Ozzy*, Rollins, **Danzig**, Fender,
Beavis, Axl, **Slash**, Judas, *Halford*, ALICE,
Gene, Kiss, QUEEN, Solo, *Ace*, Pantera,
LIZZY, Lunchbox, **Dio**, PURPLE, *Maiden*, Ironman,
Mosh, Aerosmith, Black, **AC/DC**, Crue,
Hellion, Pearl, *Sandman*, Halen, Roth,
MOTLEY, REAPER, **Korn**, **Rock Oyster**

MASTER OF PUPPETS:

> SLAYER, *PUPPETMASTER*,
> **Beast**, ***Crazytrain***, Destroy,
> *BLOOD*, ABYSS, Scream, *SPINAL TAP*,
> SABBATH, Ratt, ***MEGADETH***

NAMES FOR LOITERING AROUND THE COFFEE SHOP

Are we getting a little too weird for you? If you are looking for a slightly more typical indie name, something suitable for a kid who will be comfortable just lounging and gets the perks of being a wallflower, then this is the list for you. These names will be on many kindergarten rosters but are still pretty cool. For a name that doesn't really fit into any category but can just sit around the café for a few hours each day, stealing electricity, gazing out the window, journaling, and sipping a fair-trade cappuccino (even if most of them have nothing to do with coffee), look no further than these.

ONE ESPRESSO:

Beatrice, Isaiah, ***ELI***, Zoë, ***JACK***, Henry, LILA, Miles, *NORA*, Jude LILY, Quinn, *Kaya*, Charlotte, *STELLA*, ***AVERY***, *Riley*, Tessa, **Lydie**, MARLO, Sam, *CLARA*

TWO ESPRESSO:

WALT, *EDIE*, JOSIAH, *LOTTIE*,
Silas, *Viola*, Dezi, EVIE, *Miranda*,
Eamon, *MATILDA*, **Nico**, Frannie,
Adelaide, Hattie, *Millie*, ELOISE,
ARLO, *Cleo*, **Etta**

THREE ESPRESSO:

Tall, FOAM, CIDER, *Sofa*, **Mocha**, CRUMB,
Wi-Fi, Holler, *Trapper*, CATURRA, *WALLFLOWER*,
LAZY, Venti, *Roast*, ESPRESSO, Latte, **Moka**, *Melitta*,
PERCOLATOR

NAMES THAT WEAR COZY LEG WARMERS

If you want to name your baby something completely adorable, cute, and cozy, like Michael Cera, look no further. You just want to spend your whole day sitting around in your PJs with these names, finger-painting the furniture, watching cartoons on VHS tapes salvaged from the thrift store, and then baking peanut butter cookies for dinner while dancing along to Belle and Sebastian. Awwwwwwww!

SWEETPEA:

Birdie, *Coco*, CHARLEY, **Gus**, *Minnie*, **PJ**, MILO, **Joy**, CECE, LEIF, Alfie, *AUGGIE*, **FAY**, BENJI, *Frances*

HEART-SHAPED CIRCLES:

Juniper, *LULU*, **Billie**, *Lou*, POPPY, Mae,
TEA, **Cherille**, Cera, *DOLLIE*, *Mikey*,
HEMKEY, Monette, *ROOS*, Elio,
Oona, **ZELMO**, *IBBY*

WEARING A SNUGGIE:

SCARF, *LoveSeat*, Pookie, *Pim*, Smoochie, *PIXIE*,
Blankie, MitMit, *COOKIE*, BOOGADY, *Cozy*,
Patty Cake, *HONEY*

TIPSTER: In search of more cute names? Just comb through Jim Henson's work. From *Sesame Street* and the Muppets to *Labyrinth*, *Fraggle Rock*, and *The Dark Crystal*, Henson created dozens of the most memorable characters with awesome, snuggly names. You could fill a wacky after-school program with these fuzzy, floppy, fling-through-the-air-and-never-get-injured names: Gobo, Wembley, Mokey, Boober, Ludo, Mirk, Cantus, Feenie, Zoot, Mermer, Gillis, Herkimer, Rumple, Tosh, Doozer, Gorg, Merkey, Statler, Beastie, Roowlf, Brool, Merggle, Merboo, Mervin, Scooter, Fizzgig, Skeksi/Skek, Merple, UrSu, Hoggle, and Marjory the Trash Heap.

BOYS-WHO-ARE-GIRLS-WHO-ARE-GIRLS-WHO-ARE-BOYS NAMES

Would Abbie Hoffman have become so radical if he didn't have a girl's name? Did having not one but *two* boy names have anything to do with making Stevie Nicks just that much sexier? And would JD Samson ever have been chosen to replace Sadie Benning in Le Tigre if she didn't have such a fine mustache? WTF are we even talking about? We're not so sure ourselves—we've made the deliberate attempt in this book to avoid classifying names into genders but feel the need to point out that some names with a definite gender attachment work best when cutting against expectations.

A GIRL NAMED:

Charley, *MICAH*, Casper, **Ryan**, **ANDY**, *Dylan*, *HANK*, Ezra, Piet, *George*, Tuck, **Jack**

A BOY NAMED:

> SUE, *VIOLETTE*, **HARMONY**, *ASHLEY*, ***Ariel***, Nikki, *WYNN*, HEIDI, *Jade*, Penny, ***Lucinda***, Sandy

💡**TIPSTER:** Chicks dig gay guys—that's a fact. But they drool even more over straight indie boys who are gentle and effeminate and deep and stuff. Start your kid off with a step in the right direction by giving him a name with a gay connotation, like Elton, Pansy, Corky, or Skip . . . it may be a little hard at first, but he'll be soooo dreamy once he forms his own band.

NAMES THAT WILL RULE THE HALF-PIPE

Is there anything cooler than a skilled hardcore skater? That shaggy hair, those glazed eyes, the limited vocabulary . . . coupled with the total lack of fear of crashing on concrete or falling down flights of stairs, this makes them the original badasses. So, a little part of you dies every time you see a kid on a department-store board decked out in helmet, knee pads, and—worst of all—Nike sneakers. Give your kid a name that'll guarantee some bloody knees and elbows.

NUTS, BOLTS, TRUCKS:

OLLIE, **CALLOWAY**, Rune, **Bucky**, Losi, DECK, *Powell*, REED, PIERCY, HAWK, Stoke, *Page*, ALVA, Nollie, CARVE, McKay, Orton, **Arto**

Names That Will Rule the Half-Pipe

THRASHIN':

THEEVE, GATOR, *FAKIE*,
Riser, *RAIL*, BAM, *Lakai*,
Crate, Kubo, Bearing, **RUCKUS**,
Mullen, *TRUCKS*, Slalom,
Makaha, **VERT**, **PERALTA**,
BAIL, Tensor, *Blitz*

SKATEBOARDING IS NOT A CRIME:

Goofy, HEEL, **KICKFLIP**, **EDGE**, Thrash, *Pivot*,
PIPE, *Ramp*, Shuvit, KRUX, **Socket**, **Reflex**,
ONE8E, **THREE6T**

ONE-OF-A-KIND BABY BOOMER NAMES

You love old-fogy names, but the problem with going too far back is that many of the names are quickly and unpredictably shooting to the top of the popular lists, and you might get stuck with the next Chloë or Noah. Look at what happened to Stella and Elijah over the past few years. The trick here is to look for names that haven't come back around quite yet (and that don't rhyme with those names either) and to give your kid a name from Generation Boomer. If so, he may be the only one still standing on an original hip.

JUST QUALIFIED FOR A SENIOR CITIZEN DISCOUNT:

Valerie, CINDY, Rick, KAREN, Kathy, **Becky**, SHERRY, Mindy, CHARLENE, Darlene, **Terry**, ALAN, **RON**, DAN, Carl, **JEFF**, STEVE, Donna, *Carly*, Sandy, Debra, KEN, **Janet**, Diane

GIVE ME SOME GRANDCHILDREN ALREADY!:

GEORGE, Bob, *Dave*, *Bonnie*, *JIM*, Tim, **Judy**,
Phil, *VICKY*, Patty, Wayne, *HARRY*, *Sheila*, Dana,
BETTY, Pete, *Duane*, *VANCE*, **Dorothy**, Roy, LOU

**SO UNCOOL IT'S STILL NOT COOL BUT YOU
SHOULD MAKE IT COOL:**

LINDA, Larry, *Don*, EUGENE,
SHARON, Roger, **Gary**, *BARRY*,
Barbara, Carol

♀TIPSTER: Old people rule. They've got incredible style, blurt out the most inappropriate and sassy one-liners, and have some of the funkiest names these days. Aside from all the farting, what's not to love about them? Head to your local record shop and start sifting through the fifties section, finding names such as Howdy, Norma, Peggy Sue, Elvis, Frankie, Ginger, Jerry Lee, Maybellene, Huey, Miss Molly, Laverne, Faye, Patsy, Emmylou, Everly, Fats, and Dizzy.

NAMES FOR YOUR FUTURE EXPAT

Your child will have two choices in life: to follow your foot-steps and become a hipster-rebel, too, or to recognize the absurdity of your life choices and become an investment banker instead. Either way, this will probably result in him or her spending at least a few years in Europe—it's the ultimate indie destination and gives you bragging rights for the rest of your life. For names, we recommend staying clear of Western European names, though, as they're a bit used up—try a Scandinavian or Eastern European name, because that's probably where your kid will end up twenty years from now.

SCANDINAVIAN:

Ellif, Aasta, TROND, *JAAKKO*, MARIT, *Joonas*, *Knut*, Jyrki, *STIG*, **PIA**, Paavo, Lilja, Tilde, *Enok*, *Jorgen*, *VICQ*, Saffi, *FREJA*, LINA, *INGA*, Hannu, *Timo*, Pinja, *CLADY*, **Dagmar**, MIKKEL, **Mikko**, Jeppe, *ARLA*, *KJELL*

EASTERN EUROPEAN:

> Jenica, *OLIA*, Jasha, **Gyorgy**, DENYS, Oleksander, **YURI**, **Oxana**, Pavel, LUBOS, LIDA, *DOROTA*, **Vanda**, ***RADKA***, JIRI, *Hynek*, **VACLAV**, *AKOS*, **Gavril**, ***Lujza***, TECA, Evike, Dragos, *ELEK*, Odi, JOZSI, *BOYKA*, **BLAZHE**, MIHAI, ***Wojtek***, Rodica, *FERKO*, Vanda, *SARKA*, REMUS, BOGDAN, ***Iskra***, ***Naum***, Anca

💡 **TIPSTER:** Tied to a specific name due to a family tradition? Spice it up by using a foreign equivalent instead! John can become Gjon, Jukk, Johann, or Honzik. Susan can become Zuzia, Zozan, Suvi, or Suse. That way you can make your parents proud but still be the black sheep of the family. This works for simple nouns, as well. Love meatballs but don't want to name your kid Meatball? Plug it into Google Translate and get Cufta, Bakso, or Frikadelle instead!

NAMES THAT CAN OCCUPY WALL STREET

As a lifelong protestor, you used to think you were born in the wrong era—you should have been of age in the sixties, back when the movement mattered, when people fought for freedom, when random sex and hard drugs were plentiful. Alas, you were born in the late seventies or (even worse) the eighties. Sure, you've put in countless hours marching against Bush War One, Bush War Two, Darfur, plastic bags . . . but somehow it's just not the same. But wait! Along came Occupy Wall Street and SOPA, and suddenly voices are being heard and your weekends are spent playing board games with strangers and sleeping in parks across the United States. Why not give conformity the ultimate finger, while still remaining peaceful, by naming your kid Chase Freedom Smith or Protest War Jones? Here are some more names that will demonstrate.

Zuccotti, **Banner**, *Noam*, Bevel, *ROSA*, **CHE**, X, **NAM**, *WOLFE*, *Millard*, GLORIA, Malcolm, ARIANNA, Abbie, *King*, Ali, Liberty, LENNON/LENIN, *FREEDOM*, *Fawkes*, Taft, **SAUL**, *MARCH*, Flint, *PROXY*, **Milk**, REVIVAL, *GOVERNOR*, Kalle, **CASSIUS**, *TWEET*, Pelosi, *SPOCK*, **BRUCE**

HELL NO, WE WON'T GO:

PROTEST, CHOMSKY, **Badass**, *Butterfly*, OCCUPY, Beatnik, **B.O.**, MACE, **Civil**, ADBUSTER, Veni, VIDI, **Vici**, REVOLUTION (REV), *Declaration (Dec)*, SOLIDARITY (SOL), **COHERENT (COH)**, BONO, Facebook

TIPSTER: Feeling really rebellious? Protest censorship around the world by giving your baby a name that was banned in another country: Mafia, NoFear, Ikea, Metallica, V8, Smelly Head, Miatt, @, Stompie, UFO, Devil, Q, 89, Monkey, Dear Pineapple, Hunchback, Talula Does The Hula From Hawaii, *, Superman, Dummy, Tom, Brfxxccxxmnpcccclllmmnprxvclmnckssqlbb11116 (pronounced "Albin"), Gramophone, or Yeah Detroit. And one that surprisingly didn't get banned but is still pretty wicked: Number 16 Bus Shelter.

BAD RELIGION
BABY NAMES

No religion? We're right there with you. There are too many Marys and Josephs out there, not to mention all the Matthews, Marks, Lukes, and Johns. Even Ezekiel, Job, and Moses are making their way onto many a birth announcement these days. Boring, right? The book is longer than it looks, though (they use really thin paper), and atheists and agnostics will be happy to know that it's also full of adulterers, murderers, rapists, and corrupt kings whose awesome names have gone unused for centuries. The Old Testament is full of cursed villages, pastures, and goats with great names, too. Since you consider the whole thing a piece of fiction anyway, there shouldn't be any danger in naming your kid after one of them. And for those of you who *do* believe in something, we're sure there are still a few cool noble and wise finds in there, too; you'll just have to dig a bit deeper . . . and, of course, all that hard work will be rewarded in the afterlife.

OLD TESTAMENT HIDDEN GEMS:

> *Guni*, Mordecai, **ZADOK**, LIBNI, Uzzi, *BEKER*,
> Imna, BEZER, *HAGGAI*, **Kenaz**, Elah, *IRU*,
> **Akkab**, *UZZIEL*, **Bani**, Jeuel, *SALLU*, Eshek, **OMRI**,
> *Gedaliah*, *IMMER*, TEKOA, **ADNA**, *BOZRAH*,
> TYRE, **Sidon**, Ekron

NEW TESTAMENT STARS:

> HEROD, Titus, **ZEBEDEE**, JOTHAM, *AZOR*,
> **RACA**, Galatians, PILATE, *PERSIS*, RUFUS,
> *AQUILA*, **RHODA**, Drusilla, **CRISPUS**, LAMB
> OF GOD, Light of the World

ALTERNATIVE NATION BABY NAMES

You listened to Bright Eyes before Conor Oberst had a Mystic Valley Band, saved all your old Fugazi concert tees in hopes they'll one day fit your kid, and have already rigged it so one of your earphones is on your belly at all times—screw Mozart babies, you want to raise a baby that rocks. There are a million possibilities, but here's a playlist of some of our indie rock faves to get you started.

MODEST MOUSE:

> THOM, **KURT**, BELLE, *SEBASTIAN*, Eno, *Fugazi*, **Morrissey**, Phair, BECK, Pixie, *SEBADOH*, Sonic, STIPE, Tengo, HÜSKER, *BIKINI KILL*, VERUCA, **Tortoise**, *Portishead*, FARRELL, *POCKY*, **SPOON**, Vedder, PATTI

CLAP YOUR HANDS SAY YEAH:

Roux, Sufjan, Leon, CONOR, Cat, ANTONY, *Beulah*, *SIGUR*, *Ros*, **smog**, *DEERHOOF*, Neko, Peaches, Banjo, Grizzly, Feist, IVER, Aisler, *Rufus*, CHIK, *TransAm*, *FRANZ*, *INTERPOL*, *SHAMBLES*, HERCULES

IF YOU'RE FEELING SINISTER:

Pitchfork, *MIDI*, RIFF, Amp, *KILLER*, **MERCH**, SHIN, Knife, **Anthem**, Fender, *SUPERCHUNK*, OBSCURA, Verse, TV ON THE RADIO, *GIG*, Destroyer, *Moxie*, Bojangles, *Nimrod*, NEVERMIND, *Dirtbomb*, YeahYeahYeah, MMBOP, *LIBERTINE*

💡**TIPSTER:** Remember radio? Name your baby after your favorite high-school radio station: WBER, KLYK, KEXP, WSOU, KROQ, or SIRIUS.

NAMES THAT GET THE PARTY STARTED

Being able to plan music for a party, edgy potluck dinner, or epic road trip is an important life skill you plan to pass along to the future generation of you. Maybe you were a rising star in the club scene back in your twenties or an in-demand wedding DJ in the suburbs . . . either way, if you want your little peapod to grow up to be a real DJ, give her a head start with a name like one of these.

OONTZ:

ICE, **Amp**, *RAVE*, Disco, **VINYL**, Synth, *META*, **Mack**, SPIN, *Trance*, **Disk**, TONE, *Audio*, *SLIM*, **CHUCKIE**

Names That Get the Party Started

OONTZ, OONTZ:

Bonsai, **Bones**, Julz, *DIABLO*, Oizo, *GAINS*, CoolMic, *DANJO (DJ)*, NOIZE, **FIVE**, *BIZZY*, Grem, **CAVE**, DARI, **Judge**, *Jockey*, Mixer, *COX*, *VIJAY*, GRASSO

OONTZ, OONTZ, OONTZ:

Klyyd, EPIC, *FLEA*, **Cash$**, Cozmic, DEMP, SpinMasterTom, **VOCODER**, KASKADE, Xemper, *Hugowow*, *METL*, Meddle, **BUSY**, Xbox, DAFT, Mr.

TIPSTER: Create a mash-up baby name by taking two predictable, worn-out names and overlapping them into something fresh, ironic, and surprisingly catchy. Nathan and Alex mash into Nathalanex, Wendy and Alice become Walenicedy. Totally whack, eh?

NAMES FOR YOUR LITTLE GARDENER

That sick tomato plant out on the fire escape just isn't doing it for you anymore. Going to the farmers' market or becoming a farm share member is a little nicer, but you truly dream of a chunk of land in the country where you can just walk outside your shack, say hello to the chickens running around, marvel at the white bedsheets blowing in the wind, and then grab ingredients for a fresh lunch entirely from your gigantic garden. We can't promise interesting neighbors or a strong Internet connection, but here are some names that might get you a little closer to your dream.

Caudex, Loam, **PEAT**, ARBOR, *Bale*, Trimmer, *SPADE*, Neem, *Leaf*, Eco, **Flore**, *FILBERT*, **Aster**, Camellia, **Patch**, Rush, YARROW, **AERIAL**, Herb, *Solar*, Terrace, **Hedge**, *RAKE*, Hay, *Furrow*, Glade, LATH, *Culun*, Perennial, **LAWN**, BORAGE, *TUBER*, Espalier, ALLEE, *FERNERY*, **Orchard**, Bonsai, *Alkaline*, **CLOCHE**, **Trug**, CLIMBER, *Coir*

SOWING THE WILD OATS:

Plough, POLLINATE, **DORMANCY**,
Shovel, Sow, BULBIL, *Rooster*, Tractor,
KAILYARD, **BOTANY**, *FUNGI*, *Soil*, Potager,
SHRUB, Hybrid, **BOG**

THE INTERNET IS LEAKING NAMES

Dancing baby, sad Keanu, planking . . . memes are the true celebrities of our times, even if they're usually just made out of cat. While all the other parents are looking to their favorite music, movies, and books for the next hot baby name, find a fresher flow of names (which will probably dry out just as quickly) by naming your child after something that leaked out from the Internet instead. Or you could just name your kid Leak.

TXT:

> DERP, Meh, **LOL**, *Troll*, PWNED, **4Real**, CMON, **/b/**, LULZ, POIDH, Moar, w00t, GRAH, *Like*, TEH, NOOB, **Copypasta**, 4Chan, **Tiem**, TRIFORCE, NoHomo, **IMA**, MYEAH, **Whatevs**, *Reddit*, ASIF, **CYA**, *System32*, Tl;dr

JPG:

Plank, **Adorbz**, *Boxxy*,
LOLCAT, Sweet Jesus, HAZ, *Rage*,
FFFFFFFFFUUUUUUUU, **Magnets**,
ZEDDIE, Y U NO, RAPTOR, KEANU,
Disappoint, **UMAD**, GOATSE

WMV:

HONEY BADGER, Cone, *RICKROLL*,
NYAN, Chris Crocker, *Jessi Slaughter*,
FRIDAY, Dodson,
ALLYOURBASEAREBELONGTOUS,
RAINBOW RAINBOW

IRL:

FAWKES, Moot, **Anon**, SANTORUM, *Obey*, Bieber

LITTLE BRITAIN BABY NAMES

The British version of life is always better. Never mind the suicide rate and dreary weather—the accent and slang alone make even the most boring sentences sound fascinating. But you don't want to name your child Pippa or Immogen or Edwin like all the other pseudo Anglophiles in the United States—you know, the ones who sit around sipping tea all day, chattering on about how much better everything is in London (even though they only spent three days there in 1997). But you wouldn't mind giving your offspring a name that could carry her own show on the BBC, right? So here are some others inspired by the land that brought us the *good* version of *The Office*.

FIT FOR A CASTLE:

AGATHA, Abbey, **EMMERDALE**, Hale, Pace, Arthur, *BEADLE*, WYCLIFFE, **DOWNTON**, Hetti, DUDLEY, Merlin, **Paddington**, *Crawley*, BATES, BERYL, Drake, *Branson*, BRYCE

COCKNEYED:

> BLIMEY, **Rebus**, *McCallum*, Quid, ***BO***, DALZIEL, ***PASCOE***, HEX, *IVOR*, Jericho, *COULSON*, HILDA, *CROSSLEY*, SLAG, *Gemma*, ***PRITI***, NOBB, Eoin, ***LETTY***, Kemal, ***Pamuk***, *BORIS*, Who

COMPUTER SAYS NO:

> *CAROL BEER*, ***BADGER***, *ARSE*, CODSWALLOP, ***Filch***, *MAGPIE*, Boothe, **Allo**, Sykes, ***RAWLISON***, *CHUMLEY*, SKINT, Cleeves, *BUBBLES*, ***Innit***

NAMES HANDMADE BY ETSY

You're stylish in that subtle, old-fashioned way, and you support independent designers and crafters—so why not give your baby a name that does, too? Something that will fit in with your one-of-a-kind pleated mirror frame, your beaver-shaped cast-iron trivet, or your collection of jewelry made from vintage motorcycle parts and bottle caps . . . man, what did you do before Etsy? Here are some handmade names that will fit nicely into your curio cabinet and just might make your kid a nice profit on the side one day!

A CLASSY BROOCH:

Pearl, **EUNICE**, Emerald, LACE, *CLAY*, Jade, LOUISE, Jewel, **Floral**, **IVORY**, *HENRY*, **Esme**, ADDY, *THORA*, Frieda, **Miriam**

Names Handmade by Etsy

QUILTED BIKE SEAT COVER:

> *FENNO*, **OPAQUE**, *Slate*, *DECAL*, Botny, **ZINE**, KITT, Merio, CHAMBRAY, ***Nuno***, Bowtie, *ALOUETTE*, **Weil**, SEWON, *OKTAK*, WARBY, *AKI*, NUNO, ***ETSY***

FOX FUR LAMPSHADE:

> Crochet, **Eyelet**, ***Hem***, Deco, THREAD, Etching, *DOILY*, Hook, **JAR**, *ZIPPER*, Veil, ***Feather***, *Shell*, *PENDANT*, *Marble*, *STEEL*, *Stitch*, TCHOTCHKE, **MIRROR**, Bootsy, *Vase*

WOE-IS-HIPSTER BABY NAMES

It might seem a little morbid to name your kid after a famous suicide or depressing overdose, but c'mon, there is a well of snazzy names to be found there, and maybe your kid can pick up where her or his namesake left off. Besides, your fuddy-duddy parents and friends who would disapprove of the concept won't really know that Kurt, Virginia, or Sid refers to *that* Kurt, Virginia, or Sid. Or, if you want to be really stealth, just name your mopey artist-in-training Twenty-Seven. Ain't no sunshine anymore for these names.

KURT, **SYLVIA**, Hunter, ELLIOT, Virginia, **IAN**, Spalding, *Gray*, *ERNEST*, Dylan, Amy, **Marilyn**, *JANIS*, Bradley, **Wes**, LENNY, Bruce, DOROTHY, Zac, Abbie, **Brad**, Johnny, *Freddie*, Sid, *Jimi*, **Hendrix**, Ace, *SMITH*, Arbus, BRANDIS, *ALEXANDER*, **Ulrike**, Foster, **HAIM**, *MURPHY*, Morrison, *PHOENIX*, ANISSA, *Plato*, KEVYN, *Lester*, Jean-Michel, **Bolin**, *BUCKLEY*, **Truman**, *DRAKE*, FARLEY, *Rainer*, **MJ**, *HEATH*, MOON, *PENN*, Renfro, *EDIE*, **Hillel**, **Rothko**

OFF THE DEEP END:

> **GUNNAR**, Paxil, **Delp**, **OPI**, **Rage**, Odie,
> Sigmund, **Barbit**, ANNA NICOLE, **Jump**, Pfaff,
> MORPHINE, **Crack**

TIPSTER: If you have spent a lot of time in therapy or
were a psych major, pull out those old textbooks and check
out names of famous people in the psychology realm. This
way, you can raise a slightly less depressed little babe.
Consider Ekman, Lewin, Thayer, Keirsey, Kant, Lotze, Ellis,
Maslow, Pavlov, or Perls.

MY NAME SEEMS TO BE A VERB

Go! Run! Jump! Sometimes names that aren't names at all really do make the best choices. And how can you go wrong giving your kid an action name? You're a doer, and your offspring should be, too. What better way to keep your tot away from video games than to give her a name that *belongs* outside? Or if she is inside, at least a name that will have her crafting, knitting, reading, or ruling the world!

BABY EXTROVERT:

Hammer, *DIG*, Sway, *ZIP*, WANDER, *Skip*, Hop, Bolt, **SKATE**, SAIL, *Buzz*, TRIP, **Chase**, GALLOP, LEVEL, Hum, *MOOR*, Push, ZOOM, **SPARK**, Go, *FLY*, **Flip**, **Strut**, STROLL, *POGO*

My Name Seems to Be a Verb

BABY INTROVERT:

> **GUZZLE**, *Meander*, RUMINATE,
> GAZE, Hover, **Read**, Trace,
> **Fancy**, ESSAY, Mix, *SEEK*, KNIT,
> Say, **Chomp**, **Pop**, **Wink**, PRAY,
> FAX, Rely, RULE, Seal, REIGN,
> **Drum**, COUNT, **Beam**, CRAFT,
> **WRITE**, TYPE, Pose, SLURP, Pour,
> SEW, **GIGGLE**, Twiddle, **WHINE**,
> **Assemble**, Tinker

TIPSTER: Depending on your child's last name, it's possible that she might seem to be an acronym! Her towels will look great if you can monogram them with the initials LOL, OMG, BRB, WTF, or LMAO.

PING-PONG NAMES

Table tennis is an important sport for any aspiring subculture hero. Aside from the cool headband you get to wear—and Umbros if you're superserious—the soothing sound of the ball bouncing back and forth on the table, pinging and ponging, ponging and pinging, brings you to a higher place called the zone, soothing and relaxing yet extremely competitive at the same time. Here are some names that reflect the back-and-forth sound of this underrated sport. And, yes, it is so a sport.

ALLITERATIVE:

> *PIPPA*, *Lulu*, LILO, Fifi, **DEDE**, *Mimi*, BEBE, *Timtim*, **ZUZU**, LeeLee, **YoYo**

PALINDROMES:

> **ALULA**, *Lemel*, Cammac, **Radar**, *Otto*, Solos, *Reviver*

COOL SOUNDS:

> **Deeble**, *Doople*, Beepadee, *MOPPETY*, Blipabee, LOPADO, Doodle, **SHAZAM**, Furgle, **ZEBEDEE**

NAMES THAT DO BRUNCH

Admit it. You are a brunch enthusiast. Sure, you get a little annoyed when all the yuppie straights and their blond Abercrombie children start encroaching on the previously underrated dive diner. But come on, who can resist eating cornflake-crusted vanilla French toast or artisan breakfast pizza with a Bloody Mary on a Sunday at noon? Sometimes it really is worth the line and the caloric intake. Besides, now that you have a baby, brunch will likely be the highlight of your week, and you are going to join the throngs of brunch-going parents who annoy the crap out of the waitstaff and childless patrons. So embrace it!

ONE-HOUR WAIT:

Frenchie, COCO, **FLORENTINE**, KALE, *BENEDICT*, **MAXWELL**, Mary, *CLEMENTINE*, Clinton, *TEA*, Marge, Bart, **Miriam**, *FRIEDA*, GERTRUDE, **FRANKIE**, Poppy, MELBA, Goldie, *Lundy*

NAMES THAT DO BRUNCH

NO RESERVATIONS NECESSARY:

Rye, WHISK, Marmalade,
Mixie, COOKIE, **OAT**, Spoon, Okra,
MATZO, Berry, **Brioche**, Pumpkin,
Sieve, **HOURS**, Pepper, **Wake**,
HONEY, Challah, Raisin, ROTI, **PHILO**,
Almond, Monterey, **PAN**, Canola,
PEACHES, Coconut, Callebaut,
Souffle, TRUFFLE, Mint

CURE FOR YOUR NASTY HANGOVER:

Gravy, Bacon, Advil, Bellini, **IBU**,
Livda, Agua, Fry, **Vinegar**, FRITTATA,
Sausage, Dough, **PANCAKE**, Sugar, Scramble,
MIMOSA, TART, Chorizo, Eggie, Tater,
Bean, BLOODY MARY

NAMES FOR GADGET GEEKS

For those of you reading the ebook version of our book, thank you—we get better royalties on it! We know it's hard to focus on this paragraph without checking your e-mail, refreshing Gawker, or replying to that text message that just buzzed in, all while trying to walk down the street at the same time, but . . . hello? You still there? Hello?? Probably checking Twitter now . . . what a douche. Anyway, when you get a sec, here are some names to consider. Maybe by the time the baby is born someone will have created an app to wipe your baby's ass.

TAB, **Gadge**, Mobi, APP, Android, CAM, Ram, Giga/Gigabyte, **ONES AND ZEROES (IN-VITRO TWINS)**, **HD**, BLUERAY, Pogue, Plug-In, **Canon**, Nikon, Linux, Proxy, Wifi, MICRO, **TOOL**, Gizmo, **Google**, Bing, **Beta**, TWIT/TWEET, ZUCKER, HACK

5G ON PREORDER:

Flashmob, DoodleJump, Hybrid, **Wiki**, 00101101, Jailbreak, **+**, URL

DUDE, WHERE'S MY BABY NAMES?

All your friends asked for Camaros or BMWs for their sweet sixteen, but not you. You picked up an old 1980 Ford Pinto for $170, covered it with ironic stickers and lipstick kisses, and then stared people down whenever they gave you dirty looks at intersections. Despite leaving the doors unlocked and keys in the ignition all the time (who would bother stealing it?), you loved that damn car, more than love itself. Savor the memory of your awesome ride by passing the name to your kid.

BEETLE, Bug, **DODGE**, Geo, *COOPER*, CHEVY, *Karmann*, *JETTA*, Scooter, *PONTIAC*, Pinto, **DeLorean**, *VOLVO*, **Kia**, Audi, CELICA, *CHEVELLE*, Mazda, SMERA, *Ghia*, *PRIUS*, **Honda**, ECHO, *REV*, **RACER**, *NITRO*, INDY

PEDAL TO THE METAL:

VESPA, *RICKSHAW*, PISTON, Diesel, **ACCEL**, Torque, Drag, **Unleaded**, *UNI*, **Cylinder**, TANK, **Kymco**, **A/C**, SHOPPING CART, *YetAnotherGasCap*, **Vroooom**

NAMES THAT SMELL LIKE TEEN SPIRIT

Grunge was our original cool—our first discovery of real nonconformity. And giving your baby a name that will nod to the era that you remember so fondly will not only be stylish now but will be even cooler and oh-so-vintage in the 2030s, when your kid is twenty. Sure, it's no longer cool to never shower, and even though there has been a resurgence of nineties style, the sexiness of greasy hair, oily skin, and grime-caked clothing seems to have died with Kurt. But like all things that seem gross or weird when adults do them (farting, falling over, wearing overalls), babies can make anything cute. And heck, who doesn't love a greasy baby? Give your baby a crowd-surfing name that will bring back grunge.

ALWAYS WEARING FLANNEL:

OLYMPIA, **RAIN**, River, **PEARL**, Gavin, Alice, *STONE*, TEMPLE, *Pilot*, **WILLARD**, *Tad*

A LITTLE GRIMY:

ABERDEEN, Sonic, *Sleater*, KINNEY, **Estrus**, *Pavitt*, VERUCA, ***GROHL***, Gossard, ***VEDDER***, Pixie, *MELLON*

FULL-ON CRUSTY:

MUDHONEY, *Mosh*, *GRAJ*, PEDAL, *LITHIUM*, GOO, Scuff, ***Dishevel***, **Tartan**, *Evergreen*, *Wedge*, ***FLANNEL***, *CHORD*, Fret, **Pick**, SCRAPPY, BabyDoll, *FUZZ*, Angst, ***BRIDGE***, CREEP, Toadie, Jam, *STONER*, POSEUR, **Drear**, *PUMPKIN*, Keidis, RIFF, *HOLE*, BLACK HOLE SUN

NAMES YOU CAN SMOKE

In honor of the arrival of your little one, you have chucked your packs of American Spirits and Camel Lights and quit your other various smoking habits, too. Yay, you! But just because you've given up rolling your own cigarettes doesn't mean that you have to give up all your puffing ways. Give your kid a smoking-hot name so that every time you call it out, it'll be like finding that sole cigarette in an old pill bottle stashed in your underwear drawer that you hid from yourself the last time you quit smoking. Or, on the contrary, if you are and always have been totally anti-smoke, maybe you are just looking for a name for your little pyromaniac-in-training.

FILTERED:

EMBER, COAL, Muratti, CLOVER, *Morley*, *PERILLY*, Dunhill, BLAZE, Smokey, Philip, **MOR-RIS**, Virginia, *SALEM*, **Kent**, **Delta**, WINSTON, Lucky, MONTE, Marlboro, **WEST**, *NEWPORT*, Drum, Sobraine, **Nico**, Viceroy, SLIM, **BIC**, **CAPRI**, GAULOISES, **Esse**, Pall, KARELIA

UNFILTERED:

Charcoal, DRAG, *FLINT*,
SHAG, Arson, **FLAME**, Pyro, Smolder,
Tar, *PUFF*, **CIG**, Hash, *OPI*,
ZIPPO, *Reef*, TABAK

ONE MAN'S TRASH IS ANOTHER FREEGAN BABY NAME

When you go to the supermarket, you never bother with the automatic doors. Instead you head around back and scavenge through the dumpster—a tomato with one small bruise, a bag of potatoes with just a few sprouts to dig out, and a damaged box of elbow macaroni. Throw that in the Crock-Pot you found by your neighbor's recycling bin and you have dinner for a few nights! You *could* easily afford to buy your own food, rent an apartment, furnish it at Ikea, and drink four-dollar cups of fair-trade coffee, but instead you've walked away from the consumer cycle of work, buy, and throw away and joined the freegan movement instead. And you've even managed to furnish your new baby's nursery from all found and free items—score! Pass this tradition on to your child with a name like one of these.

LETUS, Potato/e, OKRA, Freegan,
MONTEREY JACK, Leafy, SQUAT, Stew, **BAGEL**,
Shadow, Digger, **COUCHIE**, **Muffin**, Petal, **TEDDY**,
SAUSAGEA, BLENDER, **Legume**, **Pastrami**,
JUG, **CHEDDAR**, Checker, **CAN**, Raw, FORAGE,
Pint, **Raccoon**, PIGPEN, **KETTLE**, Eggshell,
DUSK, **JELLO**, Olive Oil, Bean Curd

DIGGING A BIT DEEPER FOR:

Salmonella, **SCAV**, BRUISE, WINDOWS95,
ASSEMBLAGE, **Fatty**, Lacquer, **BEDBUG**, 2x4,
MOLD, Crock-Pot, CRACKER, **WASTE NOT**,
PBJ, SoupieDoupie, **Hives**, **Fixer Upper**,
TURPENTINE, **Cheap-O**, CASSEROLE

💡**TIPSTER:** Create your own DIY project by dumpster-diving for your baby's name. Take the first syllable from the first two or three objects you find in any trash can on the streets, and compile them into a name. A tomato and a broken hinge? Try Tohi. A yogurt cup, a busted lamp, and a used condom? Try Conyola. Feel free to fix them up, smooth the corners, and add a layer or two of lacquer to make them work a bit nicer—these could become Toey or Cronoyla, for example.

NAMES THAT ARE OUT OF THE CLOSETS AND INTO THE STREETS

Though still fighting for many basic rights in our society, gays have made major contributions throughout history, whether in or out of the closet. Socrates? Gay. The guy who saved us from the Nazis? Gay. James Dean? At least bisexual, but probably gay. Jesus? We won't even go there. Whether you're a gay parent looking to name your first child or a straight one who has given up on finding a partner and just bribed your best gay friend for his or her smart/sexy/stylish sperm or womb, give your baby a name that pays tribute to some of the great gay heroes of our past and present.

THE GAYS:

> *HARVEY*, MILK, *Genet*, Adrienne, GERTRUDE, Cocteau, *SAPPHO*, WILDE, *Foucault*, *TOKLAS*, *TURING*, Trevor, *BACON*, ACKER, *Proust*, Colette, ALIG, *K.D.*, TENNESSEE, Leonardo, *BESSIE*, Isher, Almond, Etheridge, *ELTON*, Aiken, Savage, *QUENTIN*, Ellen, *BILLIE JEAN*, *Hoover*, *DUMBLEDORE*, Priscilla, *Chaz*, *FRIDA*, Rilke, *PIER*, Gide, *RIMBAUD*, Barney, Rosie, *LARRY*, Maddow, *WALT*, SUSAN B., *Freddie*

BITCH PUH-LEASE:

> *CRUISE*, *Caesar*, Jodie, *FOSTER*, PEPPERMINT PATTY, *LINCOLN*, ELEANOR, Tripper, *SANTORUM*, *POPE*, *BERT*, Ernie, *COOPER*, *VELMA*, Travolta, *Batman*, Robin, *PIAZZA*, Spacey, TINKY WINKY, Tintin, *GAYLE*, Oprah, BIEBER

NAMES TO TATTOO ON YOUR BABY

Instead of wedding rings, you and your partner went with bands of ink instead. And now with a baby on the way, you've already scheduled a slot with your tattoo artist one week after the due date so you can get your baby's name and date of birth worked into the banner of that perfect Sailor Jerry design you've had your heart set on. So commemorate another stage of life with a name that will fit in with your overall composition.

SAILOR, Jerry, **Dice**, **TAC**, Dagger, *HARDY*, Swallow, *KANJIS*, PIGMENT, Squick, TAT, *BETTIE*, **EIKON**, Flash, Stence, *ALOHA*, Sid, *Scab*, UKIT, Uma, *ETCH*, Rollo, MOKU, Horace, *RIDLER*, *Anchor*, Rose, *TAMEZ*, OMI, **Koi**, *AITCHISON IPA*, JOMON, Dayak, **DIY**, Irons, Star, EOON, *BANKS*, Chopper, **Provon**, NEEDLE, **Inky**, *GUNNER*

YES, IT HURT LIKE HELL:

> **EPIDERMIS**, Scratcher, *SPORE*,
> **sXe**, *LAPALAPA*, Xylocaine,
> *WRASTLER*, SLEEVE, *Skull*, **Oww**,
> Autoclave, **COCKAMAMIE**

NAMES FOR A REBEL WITHOUT A CAUSE

You'd never kill, maim, or even rob someone, but you understand that a key to keeping the indie spirit alive is to go against the flow and break the law every now and then. Whether it's throwing a tag up in the middle of the night, stealing from a corporate giant, or all-out hacking a major financial institution, here are some names that will need to work hard to stay out of the slammer.

Klepto, NIMROD, *REBEL*, PETTY, *Vandal*, *ROGUE*, **Bandit**, Rascal, **HEIST**, LARCEN, Ms. Demeanor, *PYRO*, Con, *Raider*, **PIRATE**, Felon, SPEED, *CAPER*, Forge, **Loot**, SMUGGLE, **Evader**, *THIEVE*, **FILCH**, BLAG, **SCANDAL**, MOOK, *GRIFT*, Waster, MOB, *RIOT*, **VICIOUS**, **HACK**, Bloc, **NINJA**, ROB

BREAKING THE LAW, BREAKING THE LAW:

STICKYFINGERS, **JAYWALK**, *MOLOTOV*, Sniper, *BUCCANEER*, Hooligan, **SABOTAGE**, *Snitch*, VIGILANTE, **SLAUGHTER**

NAMES THAT CAN DANCE IF THEY WANT TO

Whether you're classically trained but prefer a more intuitive, fluid motion coupled with systematic breathing, or like to bounce around and make sarcastic facial expressions while throwing out exaggerated interpretations of "As Seen on TV" dance moves, or you just bop your head up and down with your hands in your pockets, gently tapping your Chucks to the beat while the band plays on, it's Friday night! You're dancing like no one is watching, but hoping of course that they are. Give your baby a name that can get into a groove.

MOMMA DON'T DANCE:

FOXTROT, *CHARLESTON*, Waltz, **Bop**, **CAN-CAN**, Frug, Twist, *JITTERBUG*, **Mambo**, FANDANGO, **FREDDY**, Jive, *MONKEY*, *Thriller*, *Polka*, **SUZIE Q**, **Mashed Potato**

Names That Can Dance If They Want To

PUMP UP THE JAM:

Krump, Crunk, **SNAP**, MOSH, Slam, *BBOY*,
BELLY, Slide, *JIGGY*, **Flail**, **STRUT**, *MERCE*,
Electro, **PEEWEE**, Pogo, ROBOT,
RUNNING MAN, SHAG, **SHIMMY**, Shake

LET'S DO THE TIME WARP AGAIN:

BOOGIE-WOOGIE, **SQUARE**, *Disco*,
JABBAWOKEEZ, **PopLockDrop**, Pelvic Thrust,
WANG CHUNG

NAMES TO SURVIVE THE ZOMBIE APOCALYPSE

Brain-bashing battle-axe? Check. Sharpened machete for decapitating heads? Check. Enough gasoline to refill your face-shredding chain saw? Double-check. In addition to these zombie-destroying weapons, you've stockpiled enough food and water to last your family nine to twelve months, guns and ammo to fend off desperate unprepared humans, and a fresh-in-the-box pair of Vans to outrun them all. Despite all this, though, you secretly long to become one of the undead, just so you can see how it feels to dig your jaws into the flesh and brains of the living, understand what it is that they really want from us, and wander aimlessly through empty yards and bleak city streets without a care in the world. Whether dead or alive, here are some names that will survive the next zombie apocalypse.

ROMERO, PLAN 9, WALKER, BROOKS, **Rage**,
BELA, Bierce, Z, DECAY, **Stumble**, LUGOSI,
Omega, **Dawn**, *28*, **Shaun**, CORPSE, **GHOUL**,
Panic, Horde, ZITS, Rot, BOMBIE, Stench,
UNDEAD, **THRILLER**, Halperin, **WANDER**, REC,
Ma, **FULCI**, Crazies, T-VIRUS, Inferi, **Decomp**,
SPLATTER, **Gilgamesh**, BLUDGEON

WORLD WAR Z HAS BEGUN:

Solanum, Zonbi, **Zombi**, NZUMBE,
DRAUGR, DYBBUK, Golem, **Mmrgh**,
Ghaaar, UUURMMH!, Brains!

EPILOGUE

NAMECHECK: TESTING, TESTING, 1-2-3

Okay, so you've made it through all the categories. We hope you've found a few names you love, thought of a few more yourself, or already decided that you found the one perfect name for your tyke and are ready to go ahead with it. Right? Wrong. The fun part is over, and now it's time to roll up your sleeves, put on your wide-framed glasses, and do some research.

When you chose the name, you probably thought that you were making such a unique choice because you don't know any other babies named Mae, Hattie, or Elmer—those were your grandparents' names. Trouble is, baby naming is like any other trend, and alterna-parents tend to all wear the same clothes, watch the same indie films, listen to the same emerging bands, and, yes, choose the same adorable names at the same time, regardless of which hipster hot spot they live in. What to do? Well, you wouldn't just show up at a venue with your band and get on stage to perform in front of an audience without doing a sound-check first, so before you spread the name out into the world, there are a few things you should do to check that the name is as strong as you think it is. Names are sort of permanent in the way tattoos are—removable, but never totally gone—so you're better off getting it right the first time around. Here's a list of things to check up on before you start crocheting the name all over yellow yarn blankets and booties.

GOO GOO GA GA GOOGLE

The most basic research tool available to all laptop-owning young parents is Google. Try Googling all the options you have thought about using so far. Try both first name alone and the full name, as well. Throwing in the middle name could help, too, because that's what your kid is likely going to go by at some point when he is a teenager and rebels against everything having to do with you. See how many hits you get when you Google your top choices, and also pay attention to what sort of people would be sharing the name. If there are fifteen results and one is the CEO of a bank and another is an annoying mainstream blogger, then maybe it's not right for you (although it could still be perfectly unique for a baby). On the other hand, if you find only coffee shops and small record labels sharing your name choices of Bindi and Blossom, maybe you are good to go. Just keep in mind, of course, that most babies don't have strong Google analytics, so this isn't a surefire way to confirm uniqueness but instead just a first step.

♀ *TIPSTER:* Typeability
Try typing out the name you chose fifteen to twenty times to see how easy or difficult it is. Does it weigh too heavily

to one side of the keyboard, like Milo or Poppy, or jump around too much and confuse you, like Clementine or Delilah? This probably won't be a deal breaker when deciding on a name, but it's definitely a benefit to have something simple to sign, such as Edie or Duke. You may also hit upon an interesting new spelling of the name if you keep making the same error over and over, liek Miek did.

SOCIAL SECURITY STALKING

You can easily access name lists at the Social Security website to see what's popular by decade and geographical area. To all you savvy name junkies, this isn't news, but it's another way to weed out choices that are way too common. Pay close attention to what is going on in your state, but also keep an eye on what names are popular in surrounding or cooler states.

PAY ATTENTION TO POP CULTURE

Television shows, movies, and music are all indicators of possible popular names. The next namecheck step is to search IMDB, Pitchfork, and Amazon for your baby's first name, see what's already out there, and then do it for the full name, too. Maybe there is a minor character who appeared in three episodes of *Dexter* with this name, so no big deal. But if it's the name of the main character in that Jonathan Safran Foer novel you never bothered to read, you can probably expect a bunch of kids with that name to pop out any minute.

USER NAME AVAILABILITY

Check its availability on major sites and as an URL. While a name like Gauge or Hopper is uncommon now, by the time your child grows up you can never be certain—it could become the next Thomas or Michael. After deciding on a name, see if it's available as a Gmail address, or as a user name on other websites your child may use one day, such as Flickr, Tumblr, Gawker, Twitter, and so on. It may be good to get a head start and reserve these for your child in advance, making a point to log on every few months to keep them current so they don't get deleted. It may also be worth the small fees to snatch the .com URL so your child can have her own website when she grows up. This could be a good tiebreaker for you and your partner—if one of them isn't available and the other is, there's a good chance that website will be more important to your child when she grows up than the name itself. Who wants to have to use an underscore every time you log on, or carry around a "437" after your name?

💡 **TIPSTER:** Once you've reserved the e-mail address, use it. Send e-mails to your baby telling her how much you laughed when she did X, cried when she Y'ed, or were worried when Z happened. Be sure to send family photos, as well, and share stories about other family members. Although she would probably prefer a car, giving her the password to this e-mail account will be the sweetest (and cheapest!) sweet sixteen present you could imagine.

VISIT THE LOCAL PRESCHOOL, DAY CARE CENTER, AND PARKS

Okay, you've done the online basics, but now you need to go where the babies are, see if there are other babies with the same name in your community, and, more important, see how the name works with other parents. Go check out the day care center you plan to one day enroll your baby in. Hint around and throw your baby's name out, and see if there is already another Derp or Diem there.

Another great place for baby-name testing is the park. You'll easily meet other young mothers out there you can test the name on. Or if you're extremely protective about the name, throw it out as if it is someone else's—"I was here yesterday and met a woman who said the same thing. Do you know her? I can't remember her name, but her little boy was named Derp. Or maybe Diem?"

You can also search around in these places to get an idea of what the other babies' names are. If there are many names that have a similar sound or vibe to the name you've chosen, this may be a predictor that the name you picked could be rising in popularity.

FINDING A NEW LAST NAME

Okay, at last you have found the perfect first name . . . but what will your child's last name be? More and more women are keeping their maiden names these days, so if this is the case, whose last name will the baby get? Or maybe you decided not to get married at all and plan to share custody but not even live together. Traditionally the baby will take the male's last name, but obviously you don't plan to follow traditional parenting methods. If one of you has a short last name that works perfectly with your partner's longer last name, or works perfectly together as the child's middle and last name or hyphenated (Kip Worthington or Flynn-Feldmann), yay, you! But unfortunately for the Tenenbaums who make babies with the Fockers of the world, naming with this method isn't so easy.

But fear not. Just because your names don't go together well doesn't mean you are doomed to never have a meant-to-be kind of life! It's actually surprisingly easy to change your last name, and there are plenty of places to look for ideas. Here are a few simple suggestions to nudge you in the right direction when searching for a last name:

- Take his, take hers, mash them together. Even two really common last names can turn into a very uncommon option when mixed—Smith and Jones become Jomith, Smones, Ithjo, Jonesmith, Mithones. You can give this one to your baby and keep your own, or rename the whole family.

- Sometimes, a little family-tree research will help you find the perfect (and fair) joint name. Maybe one of your grandmothers had an awesome or unique maiden name, like Finlay or Clemson, that goes well with both of your names. Or maybe your great-uncle's first name Quinn or Greenbriar works perfectly for a last name. If nothing else, you'll bond while poring over the family history of your partner, and you might find your future child's first name in the process.

- And of course there is the simplest, most obvious solution: You and your partner swap last names, then
have two children; one child gets your last name, and
the other gets your partner's last name. Not confusing
at all, and perfectly fair!

When in doubt, just pick something totally random. We
think that Bowie goes with everything quite well.

RENAMING YOURSELF

Now you have a first and last name for your baby, but
wait . . . you aren't even having a baby! You never plan
on having children, but your mother bought you this book in
the hopes that a cool name would change your reproduc-
tion plans. Hey, you can't blame her for trying, right? But
even if you stick by the decision not to pollute the world
with any more mouths to feed, this is the section of the book
devoted to you!

At some point in your life, it's likely you wanted to change
your name. If you have an awesome middle name or a long
name that lends itself perfectly to a cool nickname, lucky
you . . . but most of us stuck with plain names have had to
overcompensate in other areas of our lives by getting tattoos, piercings, glasses, pink hair, and vintage dresses to
display our uniqueness. It would have been so much easier
to just have been born as Elvira, Florence, or Epiphany.

Finding a new name as an adult isn't as easy as naming
a baby. For one thing, half the people in your life will insist
on still calling you Karl or Jessica, no matter what. But even

for the people who are open to your new identity, you might still want to pick something that makes the transition easier for others to remember and easier for you to transition into. The best time to do this is when you switch jobs, cities, book clubs, or brunch circles.

Certainly you could just open this book to any page and randomly pick out a new name. Or, you could turn back the pages to the "Poseurs" section in the introduction and figure out a cool new way to break up your name. You could also start going by the first letter of your name. Named Victor? V is much cooler. There's also the option of going by your initials: Kerry Lynn Evans becomes Kle . . . Allison Noel Thomas becomes Ant . . . Kaleb Sam Andrews becomes Ksa. Initials don't quite work well? You could always insert a letter in there to add to it—KleA, Fant, KsaH.

Another great option for finding a new name is to use a family name. That way, it's more likely your grandma, aunts, uncles, and parents will accept the change. They'll think it's because you have always found a kindred soul in your great-uncle Blutcher or that you think you always sort of looked like your great-great-grandmother Alma.

But this feat is not for the weak or lazy. In order to make the name stick, you will have to go in 100 percent. The best way to ensure you are never called Mary Thompson again is to legally change the name with the Social Security Administration, DMV, and LinkedIn (not that you're on LinkedIn . . . but if you are, it will find you no matter what your name is and it will automatically send out e-mail reminders to everyone in your contacts list every five seconds).

If this is a bit extreme for you, you can also opt to go

the unofficial route and simply change your e-mail and your business cards. And, if you want to be sure people remember, you can always get it tattooed on your forehead. Start a blog called "My Name Is [insert cool name here]" and send out photo announcement cards with your name next to your face . . . this will get people used to calling you Xi or Chai or Lulu. You might spend several years correcting people when they use your old name, but eventually it could take.

NAMING YOUR PETS

Pet naming, often done by children, has always been more creative and all inclusive. If you're a parent looking for good baby names, going back to your childhood pets could prove to be quite awesome—Tiger, Midnight, Diamond, Spike, Spot, Fluffy—even the most generic pet names can make cool people names.

For those of you who prefer animals over people, your cat, dog, iguana, or chimpanzee deserves to have a cool name, too. The beauty of having pets instead of children is that you never run the risk of them growing up and deciding to change their name to John or Jennifer just to spite you. Plus, you get to show off your killer name choice even more with a pet, because you'll be constantly yelling it over and over during games of fetch or when your pet reptile, Squiggy, keeps staring at you with those cold eyes.

Clearly animal and pet names work well on people, but do people names work well for your pets? We think yes. While the opposite is true for kids' names, with pet names, it is almost better when the name doesn't fit the animal at all. A few examples:

- Linda the kitten
- A fish named Mammal or a dog named Cat
- A lazy basset hound named Chipper
- A gerbil named Alexandrea
- Fluffy Love the snake

A few more pet names that rock: Duffer, D.O.G., Skippy, Spud, Pepper, Jojo, Yippy, Kip, Stripes, Mister, Storm . . .

So, whether you are having a baby or having a hamster, you can certainly apply the Pabst approach to naming anything in your life. And if you feel you are not responsible enough to have child or pet, you can always use these tips to name your car or various body parts.

BEFORE THEY WERE NAMEOUS . . .

It looks like we have come to the end of the book. Don't worry, there is still that promised bonus track! If you are still feeling like there just wasn't a unique enough option in the previous pages, maybe you should go see a therapist. Or maybe you've already successfully birthed several children and still feel like you haven't found the perfect sibling name for Armadillo and Danger. In fact, you probably only bought this book because you want to call your kid something that is not listed in any name book and you were checking to make sure your choice was nowhere on these pages. You are looking for something so damn original, man, it can't even be labeled or categorized . . . just like you. Don't worry, we get it.

So we hope that you'll be able to take the methods we suggest in this tome and apply them to coming up with your very own name. Here are some names that will get your mind greased up so you can come up with your own now that the book is finished. If you do decide to go with one of these below, we suggest burning this book right away, so you can pretend you thought of it *first*.

Ready for the grand finale of names probably never used on a human being before? Wait for it . . . wait for it . . . here it comes:

WRAAACK, PTERODACTYL, **DUMPTY**, GARRRRRRRRR, Herpdederp, **MOO**, BRONTOSAURUS, Beefaroni, HALLELUJAH, **Skyscraper**, HOLY SMOKES BATMAN, **ClipOn**, Terminator, Ravioli, **Republic of China**, Cactus, **FELT**, KOFTE, **BOCCE**, MURDERFACE, TOFFEE, ZINDER, ChunksOfLoveAndLikeAndStuff, **IRK**, **CAPPUCCINO**, Stickabook, Ouie, **FUTON**, OUCHI, Snark, **SMUG**, RICOTTA, LITTLE DEBBIE, SNIPER, PastaBatman, KLIPITYKLOCK, BRACELET, Srarp, SLOOP, Spectacle, **CANNED**, PICKLES, WIRE, **THROMP**, DIGGITY, OOMPA LOOMPA, SCHLAM, BLERK, *USA!USA!USA!*

Acknowledgments

FROM MIEK & KERRY:

First thanks go to our early champion Monika Verma—our smart, funny, savvy, talented agent at Levine Greenberg. You write a pitch letter like no other. Thanks, friend.

Second thanks go to Amanda Patten, our excellent editor, whose wit, direction, and overall coolness made Pabst a much better-behaved baby.

Big thanks to the whole Three Rivers Press gang for the enthusiasm: Meredith McGinnis, Lisa Erickson, Campbell Wharton, Ellen Folan, Jessica Wallin, Eric Fitzgerald, Cathy Hennessy, Jessie Bright, Elina Nudelman, and Tina Pohlman. And thanks to Lori Paximadis, too, for her great copy edit.

Levine Greenberg team, it sort of goes without saying, but we think we should say it anyway . . . in a book! Thank you for being such an awesome place to work. We couldn't have written this book without all the enthusiasm, feedback, and weekend use of the conference room at LGLA. Thank you, Jim Levine, Melissa Rowland, Julie Villar, Stephanie Kip Rostan, Daniel Greenberg, Lindsay Edgecombe, Beth Fisher, Victoria Skurnick, Danielle Svetcov, Tim Wojcik. Also thanks go to the wonderful Kirsten Wolf and Adriann Ranta at Wolf Literary.

Finally, we thank Elijah Bacal for naming his first six fish and unknowingly becoming the impetus for the book. And more so, to Jim Levine, for being the proudest grandparent on the planet—you seem to be matching ideas with people even when you don't know it.

FROM KERRY:

Huge thanks to all my friends, friends of friends, and random people who have knowingly and unknowingly donated names to this book.

Special thanks to my fellow name addict, Katie Harrington, for being the other half of my obsession all these years. Gratitude also goes to Michelle Brookey for the weekly phone calls that keep me sane. Katie, Michelle, maybe one day our strange-named kids will hang out watching *Portlandia* reruns in the great state of Oregon, yes?

Thanks to my wonderful family: George and Sherry Evans for the love, enthusiasm, and class rosters filled with weird names; Kelly and Kristin for being the best sisters and Nertz players in the world; and my Sparks family—David, Joni, and especially Jane, who is probably hand-selling copies out of her minivan this very moment.

And lastly, thanks to Rick Sparks for pushing me to write this book, for having good taste in baby names, and for everything else.

FROM MIEK:

I'd like to thank everyone who helped me with the book, whether by contributing ideas or just listening to me babble on about it in the process—especially to Tara, Hanne, Christa, Nathan, Amie, Rick, Ale x [*sic*], Lori, John, Caitlaegn, Mrs. Kroeckel, Fredna, and Nicci, who helped me name all those tank pets of mine so many years ago—I wasn't so great at taking care of them, but she always made sure they had great names.

And a big special thanks to my family—Mom, Dad, Rafe, Augie, Tasha, Dante, Sabrina, Lynsie, and Suzanne—I've had a lot of crazy ideas over the years and am grateful you guys have always supported them even when they made no sense whatsoever! Also, a belated thanks to my dead dog MacGyver—he was such an awesome dog; it's weird to mention the family without mentioning him, too.

ABOUT THE AUTHORS

MIEK BRUNO never plans on having children, but you should let him name yours. Before he decided to never have children, he dreamed of calling his firstborn Henceforth Therefore (or "Hen") if it was a boy or Carryon Carryon if it was a girl. Miek currently lives in Berlin, where he is the royalty manager for the Levine Greenberg Literary Agency.

KERRY SPARKS has been a name junkie since first discovering the joys of baby name books in the back corner of the mall bookstore at the age of twelve. Kerry was born in Southern California, grew up in rural Oregon, and currently resides in New York City with her husband. She works as an agent at the Levine Greenberg Literary Agency.